*with a special
section on the
environment*

WORLD MILITARY AND SOCIAL EXPENDITURES 1991

14ᵀᴴ EDITION

Ruth Leger Sivard

with
Alan Durning
and Arlette Brauer
on the environment

Franklyn Holzman
on Soviet military expenditures

D1418388

"The care of human life and happiness, and not their destruction, is the first and only legitimate object of good government."
Thomas Jefferson, US, 1809

Acknowledgements

Eleven years ago, well before glasnost opened the door to Soviet-American cooperation, two courageous physicians showed the way. Bernard Lown MD (USA) and Eugene Chazov MD (USSR), who write the foreword of this edition, established a remarkable organization, the International Physicians for the Prevention of Nuclear War. IPPNW has since become one of the most articulate and effective of the international organizations working for peace and security in the world. In 1985 it received the Nobel Peace Prize. The organization now has 200,000 professional members in 68 countries.

For insight into one major factor fueling the superpowers' arms race, Professor Franklyn Holzman, another brave pioneer, presents his critique of CIA's estimates of Soviet military expenditures.

The featured subject in the last edition of WMSE was health and in this one it is the environment. Alan Durning of Worldwatch Institute provides an interesting tour of the world's environment, highlighting the serious consequences that human activities have for our global commons. Arlette Brauer adds new emphasis to the dangers of environmental degradation, with her sobering study of the wide-ranging effects on human health. Both Brauer and Durning have suggestions for priorities for public action.

Among those contributing to the summary of military developments are: William Eckhardt, war historian; Stan Norris of NRDC on nuclear matters; Isabelle Osborne, military governments and human rights; Paul Walker, weapons pricing, technology and strategies, and Arthur Westing, arms control agreements.

Fallon Mullaney, who has been the research mainstay of this publication for the past eight years, continues to provide indispensable support. Teresa Riordan has assisted in both an editorial and research capacity. James and Susan Sivard, as always, have given help in times of need.

The final product owes its appearance to the guidance of Elizabeth Dixon, design consultant, and to Julie Schieber, who mastered control of the computer to produce the graphics.

The interpretations of the material are wholly my responsibility and do not necessarily reflect the views of the advisors or the sponsoring organizations.

Washington, D.C., March 1991

Copyright© 1991
World Priorities, Box 25140, Washington, D.C. 20007, USA

ISSN 0363 4795
ISBN 0-918281-07-5

Foreword

The unique flow of events in the autumn of 1989 ended a great divide in European confrontational politics. In 1991 the cold war is dead. Even the immoral rationale for the doctrine of deterrence no longer justifies burgeoning arsenals of overkill. Yet the nuclear arms race continues, with programs intact for weapons modernization and proliferation. Bloated military budgets are largely undiverted to long-neglected dire social needs.

The list of such needs is long and tragic. One out of every eight people worldwide lives on an income of less than $300 per year, in a state of destitution so total that it constitutes silent genocide. Over one billion people, one-quarter of the world's population, are seriously ill or malnourished. In regions of Southeast Asia, nearly 40 percent of the population is afflicted with malaria, measles, diarrheal and respiratory disease, as well as hunger. In sub-Saharan Africa, where the situation is even more dismal, 10 million children die every year of causes which are easily and inexpensively preventable.

One need not travel to the Third World. Large pockets of abysmal poverty and want exist among the mighty superpowers. In the US about 15 percent of the people lack any health insurance; 315 million have no roof over their heads; 20 million people go hungry several times a month. Yet over the past decade the US has invested almost 3 trillion dollars in the military, or $45,500 for each US family. The military investments of the USSR have been equally enormous, the economic and social situation incomparably grimmer. Both superpowers have behaved like moral pygmies, providing abundance for mighty military machines and crumbs for the needs of their own people.

Over more than a decade, Ruth Sivard has documented these egregious disparities in military and social expenditures and thereby enabled a generation of peace workers to mobilize world public opinion. The effort is far from over. Increasingly we shall be confronting crises wherein the desperately poor struggle against the wealthy for the right to decent survival and equity. With the spread of nuclear and other weapons of mass destruction, these struggles will be as dangerous in every way as the cold war.

The time for action is now. We must move more rapidly to curb the military appetite and promote the public's welfare. We must also strengthen the institutions that replace war as the age-old method for resolving differences between nations. In the nuclear era this urgent challenge must not be postponed, for delay courts global disaster.

Bernard Lown, MD
USA

Eugene Chazov, MD
USSR

Co-founders of the International Physicians for the Prevention of Nuclear War (IPPNW).
Co-recipients in 1985 of the Nobel Peace Prize on behalf of IPPNW.

CONTENTS

The purpose of this report is to provide an annual accounting of the use of world resources for social and for military purposes, and an objective basis for assessing relative priorities. In bringing together military costs and social needs for direct comparison, the report bridges a gap in the information otherwise available to the public. It is hoped that this will help to focus attention on the competition for resources between two kinds of priorities. Future issues will attempt to improve the coverage with additional measures, monetary and non-monetary, of the state of the world.

Summary

The speed of political change has been unprecedented. As citizens re-asserted control in Eastern Europe, governments gave way to the first multi-party elections since World War II. A wave of political reform also surged through the developing world. International forums were marked by a new-found harmony among the major powers.

Despite these favorable signs, the promised new era in international affairs has not yet materialized in the form of significant cutbacks in arms spending. The crisis, then war, in the Middle East made it easier for governments to resist basic changes in budget priorities. The fever for weapons modernization appears to be infectious.

Military affluence contrasts with the slowdown in world economic growth and the spreading stain of hunger and poverty. Against the Gulf threat, organized military action was swift and decisive. Against global environmental dangers, cooperative international action is slow-paced and inadequate.

Priorities 1991

The world produces enough food to feed adequately more than the current global population, but 950,000,000 people are chronically malnourished.

Since World War II prices of US high-tech weapons have increased 200-fold, and the general price level 7-fold.

A nuclear-headed cruise missile, launched from a submarine 1500 miles at sea, carries thirteen times as much TNT-equivalent explosive as the nuclear bomb that levelled Hiroshima.

Incomes of the richest fifth of the world population average fifty times the incomes of the poorest fifth.

Carbon emissions from fossil fuels have increased from near-zero a century ago to more than a ton per person today.

In the tropical forests, ten trees are cut for every one planted.

The industrial countries devote over $500 billion a year to military defense, $47 billion to aid the development of the poorer countries.

In the last 20 years over 1.6 billion people were added to the global population, while the world lost to environmental damage 480 billion tons of top-soil, essential for maintaining the food supply.

Developing countries have eight times as many soldiers as physicians.

The world's armed forces are the single largest polluter on earth; in the US they produce more toxics annually than the top five chemical companies combined.

The price of one ballistic submarine ($1,453,000,000) would double the education budgets of 18 poor countries with 129,110,000 children to educate.

Are Priorities Changing?

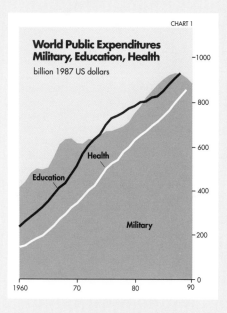

CHART 1

World Public Expenditures Military, Education, Health

billion 1987 US dollars

Health

Education

Military

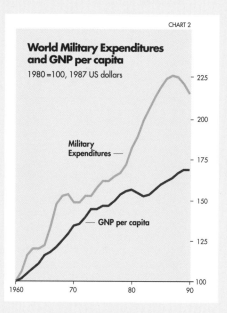

CHART 2

World Military Expenditures and GNP per capita

1980 = 100, 1987 US dollars

Military Expenditures —

— GNP per capita

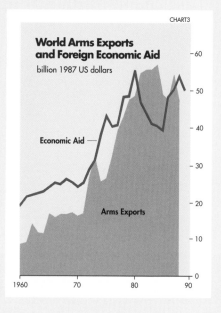

CHART3

World Arms Exports and Foreign Economic Aid

billion 1987 US dollars

Economic Aid —

Arms Exports

Neither a broad-based contraction in military budgets nor significant gains in social development are indicated by current measures of the global economy. The trend of world arms spending is slightly downward but the total decline in evidence at the beginning of 1991 is modest, and in sharp contrast to the explosive growth of recent years. Missing from the statistical picture to date is evidence of the serious reordering of priorities that could have given a limp economy the shot of adrenalin that it needs.

In a period of political ferment, preliminary global statistics on income and spending cannot be counted on to clock military and social development with any precision. They may, however, give a rough clue to the comparative pace of change. In this sense the charts above have a sobering message about the progress now underway. Even on the relatively optimistic assumption that world military expenditures will continue on a modest downward trend (in inflation-adjusted dollars), **it could be . . .**

● **8 years before the two lines on *chart 2* converge, indicating that the world's growth in GNP per capita has caught up with the growth in military spending;**

● **9 years before the world's expenditures on arms and armies are no higher than they were in 1980, before the arms race accelerated sharply;**

● **18 years before the world's arms trade drops back to the more moderate levels of the 1970's;**

● **125 years before annual education expenditures per school-age child match the current level of military expenditures per soldier.**

Perspectives

During the 1980's, militarism was king. Global expenditures on arms and armies approached one trillion dollars a year—$2,000,000 a minute. The number of wars underway reached an all-time peak; three-fourths of the people killed in them were civilians.

The decade of the 1990's opened with promise of a new era in international affairs. Public officials spoke confidently of "a new world order," presumably one turned away from military solutions and dedicated to global peace, international cooperation, and social justice.

At the beginning of 1990 there was good reason for hope. The cold war had miraculously ended. Eastern Europe basked in newly-won democratic freedoms. Long-lived regional wars in the Third World were cooling off. Among the major powers, some unilateral reductions of military forces were already underway, and more spirited international negotiations appeared to give a guarantee of momentum and permanence to the arms reduction process. The prospects looked favorable for an early and substantial peace dividend, desperately needed to offset years of social neglect.

As 1990 progressed, the rosy picture darkened. Economic, social, and environmental pressures became increasingly critical. In Eastern Europe and the USSR, severe economic shocks followed the political highs of 1989. In the developing world, where peace had seemed promising, violent civil wars sputtered on and new ones broke out. Beginning on August 2, when Iraq's tanks moved into Kuwait, the Middle East crisis became a disruptive factor world-wide, clouding the political-economic future, and in less than six months time, erupting into a major multi-national war.

As of early 1991 the chances of any quick favorable turn-around in world military spending appear to be dim. Yet there are strong underlying currents at work which could in time make a difference. Among the most important is the role of public opinion. The recent remarkable transitions from dictatorship to democracy for the most part were achieved peacefully, by the force of an awakened, determined public. Opinion polls and the press show a new readiness among the public to debate—and, if needed, to challenge—official policy on political, fiscal and even moral grounds.

In development's progress, military, political, economic, and social strands are tightly interwoven, but when the people are sufficiently engaged, history suggests, the extremes of militarism, poverty, and social neglect begin to fade away. This report, with a brief summary of what has been achieved and what remains to be done, is a reminder for them.

Political—The spread of multi-party democracy within countries and a new recognition of collective security among countries were two outstanding and positive features of the political scene in 1989 and 1990.

In Eastern Europe, including Yugoslavia and even reclusive Albania, the public regained a measure of political control as they held or planned their first free elections since the end of World War II. The pro-democracy movement, which had started earlier in Latin America, also swept into some of the autocratic societies of Asia and Africa. Young people, especially students, often took an active role in galvanizing public protests. Countries as diverse as Mongolia, Nicaragua, Gabon, Bangladesh, Benin, and Algeria—in all, more than a dozen outside of Europe—moved toward multi-party democracy.

A revitalization of the United Nations was a sign that the sense of global community had also heightened. With the USSR as a strong supporter of an enhanced role for the UN, the international organization took on responsibilities both as a mediator in conflicts and as a guardian of peace once it was restored. The five permanent members of the Security Council, in an un-

> *"Politically, this was not just a calendar year but a light year in the history of the world. The cold war, with its accompanying stress, psychoses, and anticipation of disaster, is no longer a part of our life."*
>
> *Edward A. Shevardnadze*
> *USSR, 1990*

A short selection of 1990 news items illustrates the cross currents at work in a rapidly changing military environment.

Cooling Off	Heating Up

Cooling Off

Brazil and Argentina signed an agreement not to manufacture nuclear weapons.

Ending a chill which for some lasted four decades, neighbors are taking steps to normalize trade and other contacts: N. Korea and Japan, USSR and S. Korea, Mongolia and China.

Among NATO plans to reduce force levels, UK and Germany will cut armed forces about 20 per cent by 1995, US about 25 per cent.

North and South Yemen were reunited in May 1990; East and West Germany in December 1990.

Angola's government accepted in principle a peace plan to end the 15-year civil war against UNITA, the US-backed rebel force.

Major troop reductions underway in eastern Europe included a cut of 500,000 in Soviet forces.

Five West Africa nations formed a peacekeeping force to try to halt Liberia's civil war.

Bowing to environmental opposition, the USSR suspended nuclear testing for almost one year.

The US stopped production of binary chemical weapons.

Heating Up

China and Japan are increasing the size of their naval fleets.

Military restlessness throughout South America is testing the democratic revolutions that swept the region in recent years.

Estimates of the potential tide of refugees fleeing to western Europe from economic hardships in eastern Europe run as high as 30 million.

Pakistan's nuclear weapons program accelerated during tension with India in spring 1990.

Troops in Burma arrested opposition leaders, lessening chances that the military government will hand over power to the democratically elected officials.

A coup attempt in Argentina was its fourth in three years.

Guerrilla violence was on the rise in Colombia, Peru, Somalia and Rwanda.

Stationed in the Persian Gulf area as the war against Iraq began was a US nuclear-capable fleet with 700 nuclear weapons.

Civil strife made 1990 one of the most violent years in recent history for India: at least 3000 were killed.

---

usual demonstration of harmony, agreed unanimously on action against Iraq's invasion of Kuwait.

Meshed with these positive political trends were ominous signs of increasing tensions and civil strife. New freedoms, the rapidity of change, and raised expectations apparently released ethnic, racial, religious, and tribal animosities which had been dormant or suppressed for years. From South Africa to India and Eastern Europe explosions of violence threatened domestic stability. In efforts to avert political fragmentation, several countries, the USSR, Yugoslavia, and Czechoslovakia among them, loosened central controls, but threats of breakup and/or civil war remained. As 1991 opened it was clear that the trends toward greater political democracy would not follow a smooth path, nor necessarily a peaceful one.

Military—In some respects military developments in 1990 mirrored the radical political changes underway. The breaching of the Berlin Wall in November 1989 proved to be an appropriate symbol of breakthroughs affecting both military power and active hostilities.

The most striking influence on the arms race was the continued warming of East-West relations in Europe. As each of the two major military alliances, the North Atlantic Treaty Organization (NATO) and the Warsaw Pact, lost its principal enemy, conventional military forces stationed in central and eastern Europe began to shrink. Starting as unilateral withdrawals and cutbacks by the USSR, the reductions were reenforced by progress on the first treaty agreements controlling conventional arms. By December 1990, the military fears of half a century had been largely dissipated and NATO could say of the Warsaw Pact that "we no longer see each other as adversaries."

The ending of the cold war also had constructive effects far from the European front. The two superpowers joined in efforts to bring peace to Afghanistan, Angola, and Cambodia. In addition, there were indications that the covert external support which had helped to prolong other Third World con-

flicts was declining. A favorable sign was that in 1990 the number of wars and the number of deaths in wars had dropped for the fourth successive year.

Collective security also made some advances in the military field. The enormous force marshalled in the Middle East against Iraq represented an unusual coalition of over 30 countries from six continents, united by the common objective of reversing aggression. As an alternative to war, the Security Council of the UN put into effect a trade embargo against Iraq which in scope and national participation was also unique. The coalition's ships helped to enforce it. Before the effectiveness of economic sanctions could be fully tested, however, hostilities started on January 16, 1991.

The various factors affecting national military programs in 1990 had relatively little net effect on global military spending. The mild contraction in expenditures which began after a peak in 1987 shaved the increase over 1980 to about 20 percent by 1990. This meant that estimated global military expenditures, after adjustment for inflation, were still more than 60 percent above average annual outlays in the 1970's and twice as high as in the 1960's. Other military indicators—armed forces, arms trade, nuclear inventories—remained at or near peak levels. Spending for military research began to drop in real terms, but continued to dominate government research priorities.

More encouraging than this statistical record was the further progress by the major military powers in disarmament negotiations. The conventional arms treaty (CFE), imposing strict limits on forces in Europe, was signed by 22 countries in November 1990. Signing of the strategic arms reduction treaty (START) was planned for a summit meeting in early 1991.* Among other treaties under discussion were short-range nuclear weapons, armed forces, and chemical weapons. While the US continued to hold out against a comprehensive nuclear

---

* The summit was postponed, presumably because of the Gulf crisis, but there were also some unresolved political issues. As of March 1991 no new date had been set.

test ban, the number of nuclear tests by all nuclear powers did drop sharply in 1990, reaching the lowest level since 1960, when there was a temporary US/USSR moratorium.

Economic—The growth of the world economy in 1990 was slower than it had been since the recession of the early 1980's. Industrial states made a fair showing but the economies of the USSR and Eastern Europe took a nose dive as they struggled with the painful adjustments needed to move from rigid centralized control to functioning free markets.

The oil-importing developing countries were particularly hard hit by the jump in oil prices associated with the Persian Gulf crisis. Among developing countries in general, the increase in gross product in 1990 was barely enough to keep up with rapidly growing populations. In most of the poorest countries per capita GNP growth was negative, and poverty ever more pervasive.

It was the economic crisis in the USSR and Eastern Europe, however, which made the headlines world-wide in 1990. As unemployment lines and food shortages grew, and prices increased sharply with the removal of government subsidies, the public's initial euphoria dissipated and protest and disorder were on the rise. In the turmoil of the early transition period, it was not yet clear whether countries choosing the quick route to private enterprise, or those making a graduated adjustment were likely to be more successful ultimately in achieving economic progress with social equity.

What was clear about the situation in Eastern Europe was the danger of economic breakdown in the region and the need for external assistance to prevent serious repercussions throughout the global economy. Faced with a rush of refugees from the east and a threat to its own stability, Western Europe led in marshalling the aid which began to flow east in 1990.

There was no immediate indication that meeting Eastern Europe's emergency needs would necessarily shrink the year's economic assistance to the Third World, although some countries would be hard hit by Soviet cutbacks. In 1989, the latest year available, foreign aid in real terms declined slightly. In view of the perilous economic situation in the poorest countries, the industrial states were under pressure to double their aid. In 1989 they had given a modest 0.33 percent of their GNP.

Like the pro-democracy movement, collective economic security in the Third World seemed to take momentum from developments in Europe, where the 12 members of the (western) European Community were making rapid progress toward the goal of economic union by the end of 1992. In Latin America and Asia officials discussed strategies for both technical and economic cooperation to revitalize their common markets. Except in Eastern Europe and in the Middle East, a spirit of regional cooperation seemed to be in the air.

Social—In the developing countries particularly, the continuing challenge was not simply economic growth but social development. Even in the mid-1980's when growth was advancing more briskly, it was evident that development progress, with its broader objectives, did not flow automatically from an expanding economy. Development, as is now generally agreed, should promote social equity; that is, alleviate poverty, provide employment, satisfy basic needs. In meeting these terms, 1990 was no more successful than previous years.

The gap in per capita income between developed and developing countries continued to widen. The richer countries had, on average, 20 times more income per head than the poorer. Beyond disparities such as these, the staggering reality of the world of 1990 was the number of people living out their lives in unrelieved poverty. International agencies estimated that more than one billion of the world's 5.3 billion people had incomes below the poverty line. In the 41 least developed countries in the world, per capita income averaged less than $250 a year, and was deteriorating rather than improving.

Various statistical measures other than income levels testify to the appalling deficiencies in global development at present. In the modern world, with its abundance of resources, a shelter, clean water to drink, adequate food for an active working life, basic health care and basic education, should be a human right. Few countries, including some of the biggest military spenders, have safety nets that are wide enough for protection of this scope. The yearly deficit in terms of human development continues to grow. It reflects a tragic distortion of

The numbers stand in long rows like tombstones, monuments to the lives lost to society's neglect.

500,000 women die in childbirth

700,000 children are blind due to vitamin A deficiency

600,000,000 have incomes under $300

146,000,000 children 0-4 years

children paralyzed by polio

1,500,000 women have AIDS virus

3,500,000 children die of dehydration

14,000,000 children die yearly of preventable disease

10,000,000 malnourished women bear malnourished babies

20,000,000 babies are born dangerously underweight

14,000,000 children die before they are five

100,000,000 people have no shelter

1,500,000,000 lack primary health care

600,000,000 women have nutritional anemia

900,000,000 adults are illiterate

200,000,000 have iodine deficiency

1,500,000,000 have unsafe drinking water

950,000,000 are chronically malnourished

1,100,000,000 live in poverty

2,900,000,000

priorities in a world where military power has been given first call on public policy and public budgets.

Over the 30-year period shown on *chart 1,* page 6, total military expenditures (in constant 1987 dollars) amounted to two trillion dollars more than public expenditures for all levels of education, six trillion dollars more than expenditures for the health care of a rapidly growing, largely unserved, population. The Third World, with three-fourths of the world population, accounted for less than 10 percent of global education expenditures, for no more than 5 percent of world health expenditures. It is not surprising, therefore, that it is these countries that have most of the world's poor and adult illiterates, that their infant mortality rates average five times higher than in the richer countries, their life expectancy 12 years shorter.

Environmental—The 1980's had been a decade of increased environmental awareness among the world public. In 1990, as new evidence of dangerous environmental conditions helped to heighten public concern, there were also signs that political action to contain environmental damage was on the rise.

Rather belatedly, but now with more unanimity, governments and international agencies agreed that safeguarding the environment should be an intrinsic feature of development planning. Population pressures, environmental degradation, and poverty were recognized as inseparable problems for both developed and developing countries.

The links showed clearly in Africa, where foreign aid to cover basic food needs was taking a growing share of development assistance. The overuse and misuse of resources resulting from fast-growing populations had impoverished the land. Erosion, desertification, and chronic droughts were creating serious food shortages and waves of "environmental" refugees, people who could no longer meet their food needs where they lived.

In comparison with the serious deterioration of the environment, international efforts to halt environmental degradation made progress slowly in 1990:

▪ A landmark achievement was a treaty designed to protect the ozone layer, which shields the earth from dangerous ultraviolet radiation. Signed by 93 states, the treaty will phase out production of ozone-depleting chlorofluorocarbons (CFC's) by the year 2000. The treaty also established a fund to assist Third World countries to protect their environment while expanding their economies—an important recognition by the richer countries of the need to assist the poorer in dealing with environmental problems affecting health.

▪ In November 1990 the 70 signers of the 1972 Dumping Convention extended the agreement to cover a halt in ocean dumping of industrial wastes.

▪ On world climate control, considered a critical issue for international action, no agreement was reached at the World Climate Conference in November 1990, but 22 industrial nations other than the US committed themselves to stabilize or cut back emissions of carbon dioxide, the major culprit in global warming. The 135 countries attending the conference agreed to begin negotiations February 1991, with the goal of a global treaty by mid-1992. No one expected this to be an easy task.

Beyond national and international laws to control environmental damage, there was further progress on an interesting international effort to develop the means of measuring the value of environmental resources (a forest or a mineral, for example) and the cost of use or damage to these resources. "Green" accounting will give planners a better understanding of the relative price of such ecological time-bombs as pollution, global warming, and deforestation, and the price of actions to prevent or remedy them. It can link the environment to a country's economic activity and lead to a different, more realistic concept of economic development, which is currently measured by gross national product (GNP). Water, land, air, trees are assets, consumed and perhaps depleted in the process of economic activity. Giving them value and depreciation will make more visible the extent to which development is or can be sustainable as well as equitable.

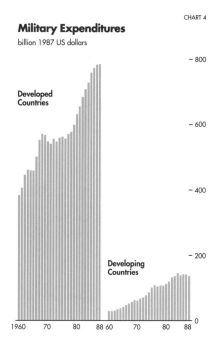

CHART 4

Military Expenditures

billion 1987 US dollars

The developed countries continue to account for the great bulk of world military expenditures. Their spending amounts to 85 percent of the world total (*chart 4*).

But when these expenditures are measured in terms of income equivalents (*chart 5*), it is the Third World, with per capita GNP averaging only 5 percent of that of the developed countries, which carries the heavier burden by far. Despite some retrenchment in military spending recently, their annual outlays still take the equivalent of 180 million man-years of income, vs. 56 million man-years for the developed countries. In other words, the burden of the arms race in relation to income, is more than three times greater in developing than in developed countries.

CHART 5

The Burden of Military Expenditures in Equivalent Human-Years of Income

million

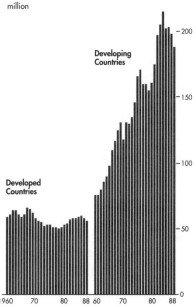

Military Burden

The world arms race continued at high speed in 1990. Preliminary data indicate that total military expenditures were about $880 billion (in 1987 dollars). In inflation-adjusted terms, this would represent a dip of 5 percent since the peak in 1987. Although down slightly, expenditures in 1990 still ranked among the largest military outlays on record, exceeding annual totals in constant dollars in all but five of the past 30 years.

Spending at these levels sustains an impressive military structure. The world now has 26,000,000 people in the regular armed forces, another 40,000,000 in military reserves, a stockpile of 51,000 nuclear weapons, 66 countries in the business of peddling arms, 64 national governments under some form of military control—and 16 wars underway.

These dimensions of military power are significant because they convey endurance and stability to military budgets. They suggest why the ending of the Cold War did not promptly produce an appreciable drop in global expenditures. Apparently that will take longer, and more public pressure.

Meanwhile it may be useful to search out historical and other perspectives on the arms race: the economic impact it has, the resources it commands, the technology it has created. How does it affect the public it is intended to protect? What keeps it going?

Impact

The economic costs of military expenditures for society can be measured in several ways, among them:

● *As a percent of gross national product (GNP)*
The shorthand indicator most commonly used is the ratio of spending to the world's GNP. This can be misleading. Expressing military defense as a share of GNP may inadvertently give an impression that it should keep growing as the economy grows; in other words, a ratio that is stable over time can appear to be a favorable sign. There is, in fact, no apparent reason why the military threat to a nation should grow as the nation becomes richer. Yet 65 of the 142 countries in the WMSE statistical record seem to say that it does—since they have maintained or even increased their military-to-GNP ratio with the growth of their GNP since 1960.

● *As a burden relative to income per capita*
The charts opposite give another view of impact, indicating that it is relative to ability to pay, and therefore can best be represented not by GNP alone but by GNP per capita. Both developed and developing countries have in recent years spent 5–6 percent of their GNP on military programs. For the poorer countries this fraction obviously yielded a much lower military outlay in dollar terms (*chart 4*). However, as *chart 5* shows, the economic impact of their military expenditures was far heavier. At 1988 levels of GNP per capita, the Third World lost to the arms race in a single year the equivalent of 187 million human-years of income. In these terms, the countries least able to afford it bore the major share—close to four-fifths—of the world's military burden. The arms race clearly has been a formidable barrier to their needed development.

● *As public wealth spent*
An assessment of impact can also be made in value terms, in billions of dollars. The heavy weight of military outlays on the global economy then becomes clearer. Since military spending is not growth-producing, as expenditures on education, health, infrastructure would be, the economic burden is cumulative. Even a small but steady drain of productive assets becomes a major loss over time. Thus world military expenditures from 1960 to 1990 add up to $21 trillion ($21,000,000,000,000) in 1987 dollars, equivalent in size to the value of all goods and services produced by and for the 5.3 billion people on the earth last year.

● *As opportunities lost*
Another way to look at economic impact is in terms of "opportunity costs", or the value of the alternative productive uses of the resources which are foregone in the drive for military power. An example would be the equivalent investment in human capital to provide schooling for hundreds of millions of children who had no schools to go to. Aside from the immediate benefits this investment would provide for the

> *"An increase of one year in average years of education may lead to a 3 percent rise in GDP."*
>
> *World Bank, 1990*

recipients, educated children would in turn make a greater contribution to the world economy, increasing the economic product and its growth, to the benefit of all.

The example represents the numerous opportunities lost to social development in an era of military growth. It suggests that the true burden of the arms race goes far beyond the direct financial outlay which supports it. Even without their use in war, weapons have a cost in lives lost.

Historic growth—The military expenditures of 1990, like the weapons they buy, bear little resemblance to the war department budgets of 50–60 years ago. In size and sophistication, the military establishments that exist today are a comparatively recent development. A look back gives some idea of the scale of the changes which have occurred.

Before the mid-1930's, when national budgets began to rise in response to the Hitler threat, the total annual outlays of all governments for their war departments are roughly estimated, based on League of Nations figures, at $4.5 billion. In the prices of today, these expenditures may represent as much as $50–60 billion. But now the world spends close to $900 billion a year, suggesting at least a 15-fold increase in the importance governments attach to military power.

By comparison with demographic and economic change, the growth in military expenditures is sobering. The jump in spending vastly exceeds the 2.6-fold increase since the 1930's in world population, i.e. in the number of people to be defended. Growth of military spending in comparison with growth of the world economy over those years is more difficult to document statistically, but it can be noted that the US, which was the largest military spender in the early 1930's and is the largest today, then devoted 1 percent of its GNP to military budgets and now spends over 6 percent of its much bigger economic product.

War itself must be considered partly responsible for this revolutionary change in the dimensions of military power. After World War II, world military spending did not return to pre-war levels, nor did it do so after the smaller wars that followed. Analysts have sometimes described this phenomenon as the "ratchet effect." Two factors created by war tend to push the action to higher than normal peace-time levels after it has ended: one is the war-time growth of the military-industrial complex, and the other the acceptance by the public of a higher level of sacrifice, to which war had accustomed them. Without organized and persistent public resistance, the military establishment created to meet the emergency tends to remain in place—a tendency which should be of some interest to the citizens of the 40 or more countries whose forces are engaged in wars as of January 1991.

CHART 6

Government Expenditures for Research and Development

billion US dollars

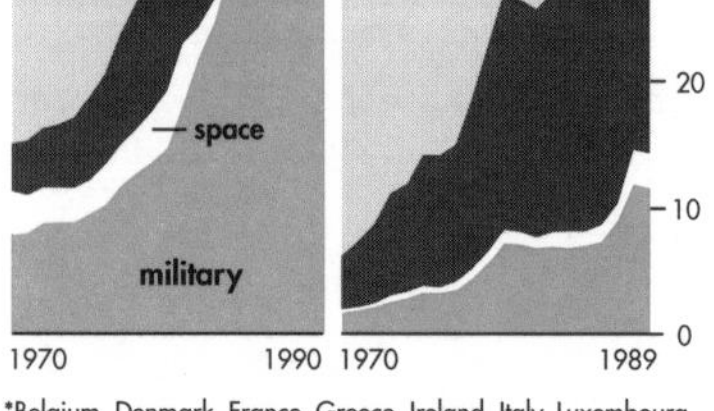

United States
European Communities*
civilian
space
military
70
60
50
40
30
20
10
0
1970
1990
1970
1989

*Belgium, Denmark, France, Greece, Ireland, Italy, Luxembourg, Netherlands, Portugal, Spain, United Kingdom, West Germany

> *"In recent years, as military hardware has become more exotic, no decisive technological spinoffs have emerged."*
>
> *Kosta Tsipis US 1990*

Dangerous Security

Stimulated by the demonstration of the awesome power of two nuclear bombs in World War II, military programs in the postwar period moved quickly to an intense competition in research and development (R & D). The results of the research gave an irresistible momentum to the arms race. They also changed the face of warfare—the speed and accuracy of weapons, their range, efficiency, and above all, their incredible destructiveness. The technology created in the name of "security" is now capable, if unleashed, of ending life on earth.

Research—The actual outlay for weapons research is a relatively small fraction of the total funds that governments devote to military preparedness, but its growth since World War II has been even more spectacular than the overall rise in military expenditures. A clue to the investment involved can be gleaned from US budgets since the war.* In fiscal year 1947 the US spent a total of $1.7 billion on military-related research, and in fiscal 1990, having cut back slightly since 1987, it was spending $26.1 billion (comparisons expressed in 1980 prices). The rate of increase in R & D spending was almost four times the rapid growth in total US military expenditures in that period.

As *chart 6* indicates, in the US (and undoubtedly in the USSR as well) government expenditures for military R & D dwarfed those for all civilian needs combined. While the superpowers put their major effort on weapons technology, the industrial countries of western Europe, as well as Japan, were concentrating on the technology that would keep their basic industries competitive in world markets. The economic results, as evidenced in the relatively slower growth of industrial productivity by the superpowers, are illustrated in *chart 14*, p. 27.

Technology—The huge annual investments in military research paid off in a technological advance in weaponry that has no counterpart in the civilian field. The results, in terms of increasingly deadly instruments of war on land, in water, air, and space, are nothing short of spectacular.

Price comparisons give some clue to the upgrading which has occurred. The US price index for all goods and services averages seven times higher than at the end of World War II.

*The two superpowers together clearly have dominated the R & D competition but reliable budgetary figures are not yet available for the USSR and its effort must be judged from the technology it has produced; in many respects it has kept pace with the US.

For weapons, however, cost increases of 200 times or more (for a weapons system with the same general name and function) are not uncommon. Among the American armaments in use in the war against Iraq, the price of an army tank, at $4,400,000, is 88 times higher than its World War II counterpart; a bomber, at $28,400,000, is 130 times higher; a ballistic missile submarine, at $1,453,000,000, is 300 times higher; a Stealth fighter, at $106,000,000, almost 2,000 times higher than the World War II fighter. If comparable price increases had occurred in the civilian market, the average family automobile would now have a price tag of at least $300,000.

Price rise does not necessarily guarantee equivalent quality gain. Waste and fraud in the arms business drive up prices. Structural and operating defects which show up in tests, gold-plating, cost overruns, exceptional profit margins, are all too common in a business with sales exceeding $100 billion a year. Between 1970 and 1989, purchases of military equipment by the NATO countries alone averaged over $70 billion a year in 1987 dollars.

Conventional weapons—Despite waste and inefficiency, spectacular advances in weapons technology are undeniable. Two aspects of the technical revolution are illustrative of the changes which have occurred in the weapons that are called conventional:

• One is range coupled with precision guidance. The emphasis is on computerized radars, remotely-piloted vehicles, laser- and television-guided bombs. Satellites and airborne radar can see far into enemy territory. Targets can be destroyed from great distances. A plane flying at a height of 40,000 feet can hit a target on earth with remarkable precision. A soldier firing a wire-guided weapon can destroy a tank two miles away. A submarine submerged 120 miles at sea can pinpoint a land target with a missile which is guided by the terrain map in its nose. In the war against Iraq in early 1991, the smart bombs and precision-guided missiles quickly established the coalition's air superiority.

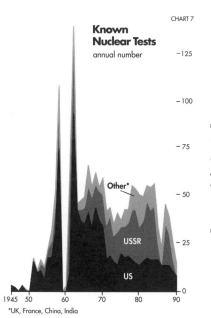

Known Nuclear Tests
annual number

CHART 7

Other*

USSR

US

1945 50   60   70   80   90
*UK, France, China, India

"The [nuclear] industry is a great deal more dangerous than you are being told."

**Dr. Alice Stewart
UK, 1990**

Precision targeting presumably has an advantage for the recipient as well as the sender. Military proponents argue that it makes for a more humane attack, directed at military targets, avoiding the carpet (saturation) bombing used in Vietnam and the fire-bombing and firestorms of Dresden and Tokyo.

• On the other hand, the capability for massive destruction has also been markedly improved. In one sortie a bomber can drop 50 or more bombs of 500–1,000 pounds each. Explosive power has been greatly enhanced. A single cluster bomb detonates into several hundred bomblets. Fuel air explosives disperse fuel into the air and then detonate the fuel cloud. Both in lethality and in area covered, so-called conventional weapons today approach small nuclear weapons in destructive power.

What this means for the noncombatant, especially in urban areas where dwellings are mixed with military targets, is that the battlefield now surrounds and engulfs him; there is nowhere to hide. Conventional arms increasingly take on features of massive destruction. They are inhuman as well as indiscriminate in their effects, virtually guaranteeing that in war civilians will be the major victims.

Nuclear weapons—Far beyond any of the technological marvels that conventional weaponry has yet been able to achieve is the destructive force inherent in nuclear weapons. Constant testing (1,814 tests since 1945) has fine-tuned the art of potential nuclear devastation (*chart 7*). Not only has the efficiency of nuclear warheads been radically improved, but also the variety, speed, and accuracy of the means of delivery.

Increased efficiency means that mini-nukes are now possible. The gravity bomb, Little Boy, which was dropped on Hiroshima, weighed 9,000 pounds and carried 15,000 tons of TNT-equivalent explosive, killing or maiming 200,000 people in one explosion. Now, with the improved yield-to-weight ratio, nuclear warheads can be incorporated in artillery shells with a weight of 95 pounds and a range of 18 miles. These have a yield of 2,000 tons of TNT equivalent. More powerful is the nuclear-headed cruise missile which weighs 2,650 pounds. Launched from a submarine at sea, it can travel 1,500 miles under its own power, and release up to 200,000 tons of explosives on the target. Far more powerful, of course, are the intercontinental ballistic missiles, which travel 8,000 miles at an incredible speed of 15,000 miles per hour, loaded with multi warheads and enough explosive force (up to 5,900,000 tons of TNT, over 300 times the power of the Hiroshima bomb) to destroy not just one but several major cities.

In the 45 years since Hiroshima the nuclear powers have built up a mind-boggling stockpile of nuclear weapons. At the height of the superpower competition, the US and USSR between them had an inventory of 56,400 of these weapons.

(continued, page 16)

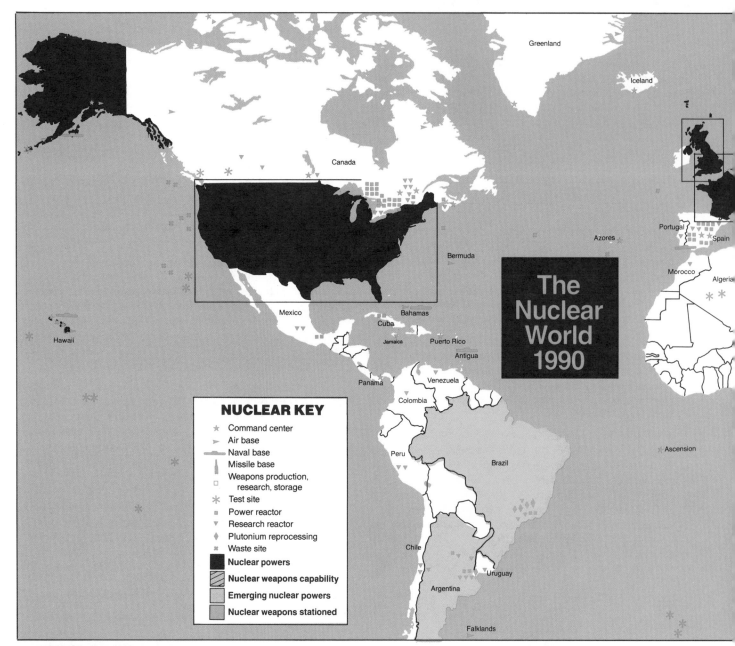

The Nuclear World 1990

NUCLEAR KEY

- ★ Command center
- ➤ Air base
- ⚓ Naval base
- ▮ Missile base
- □ Weapons production, research, storage
- ✳ Test site
- ■ Power reactor
- ▼ Research reactor
- ♦ Plutonium reprocessing
- ✺ Waste site
- ■ **Nuclear powers**
- ▨ **Nuclear weapons capability**
- ▯ **Emerging nuclear powers**
- ▮ **Nuclear weapons stationed**

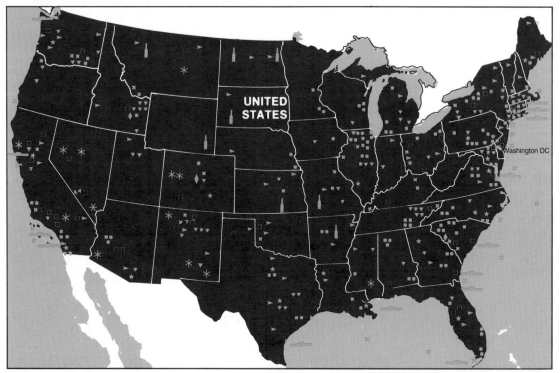

UNITED STATES

Washington DC

Spreading Nuclear Poison

The nuclear map continues to grow more crowded and more dangerous. It is now populated by 51,000 deadly nuclear weapons and by 857 nuclear reactors. To perfect the weapons, 1,814 nuclear tests have been conducted since 1945.

Only six countries (US, USSR, France, UK, China, and Israel) are considered full-fledged nuclear weapons powers, but clandestine programs are increasing, and South Africa, Pakistan, and India are believed to be on the threshold of acquiring nuclear weapons, if they have not already done so.

In addition to the land-based nuclear network, nuclear weapons are carried by 745 ships and submarines, which quietly, secretly, circle the globe with their life-threatening cargo.

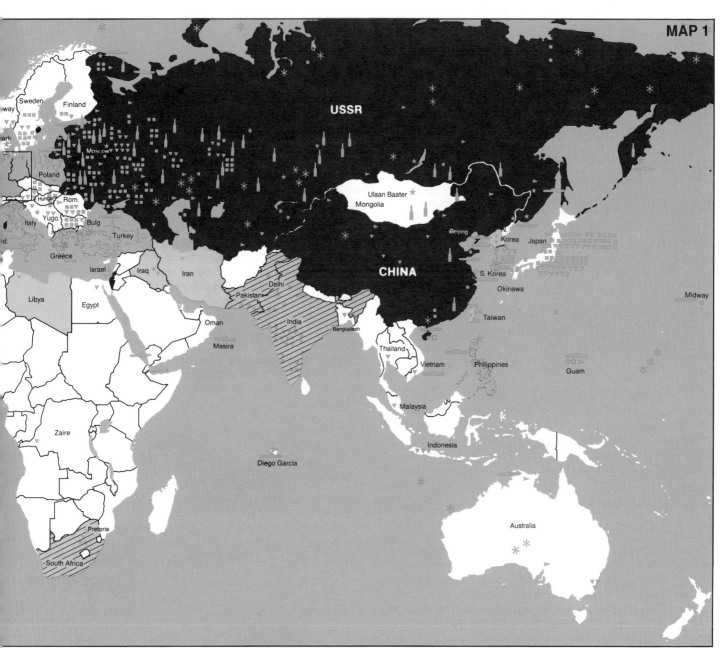

MAP 1

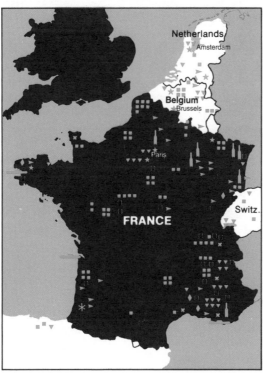

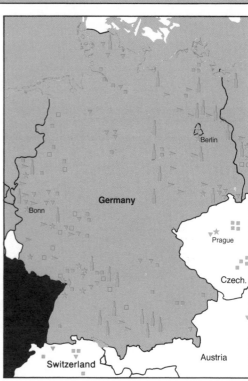

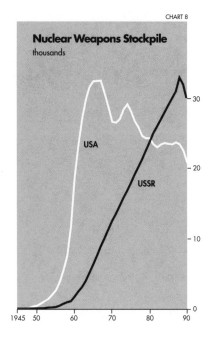

CHART 8

Nuclear Weapons Stockpile
thousands

USA

USSR

30

20

10

0

1945 50   60   70   80   90

Reflecting arms control agreements and other pressures relating to safety, budgets, and public opinion, the superpowers' nuclear stockpiles have begun to decline. They still represent an incredible overkill.

They have since shrunk by 10 percent (*chart 8*). With 52,000 weapons still in the stockpiles of the six nuclear powers, this arsenal remains formidable, and dangerous in the extreme, representing an explosive force *1,600 times* the firepower released in three major wars (World War II, Korea, and Vietnam) which killed 44,000,000 people.

Aside from the obvious excess of killpower represented by these weapons, with their threat of planetary catastrophe if they were ever used in war, the nuclear arms race poses an unusual risk to civilian health and safety even in peacetime. In the process of producing the weapons, testing, and transporting them, public officials have ignored and compromised the public's security to a degree unknown in other activities except possibly war-making. For decades secrecy was used to conceal the dangers inherent in the nuclear industry. It took two nuclear disasters (at Three Mile Island in the US in 1979 and Chernobyl in the USSR in 1986) to awaken public concern.

Sacrificing Lives to Defend Them

Civilian insistence has only recently broken through the barriers of official secrecy. The result has been a continuing series of shocking disclosures of nuclear dangers to the environment and the public's health. A sampler drawn from the press is illustrative.

• At the main Soviet test site, near Semipalatinsk, strong grass-roots pressure, combined with evidence that cancer rates were 70 percent above the national average, forced authorities to cancel nuclear testing at the site.

• The cost of cleaning up potentially lethal waste at the US radiation-contaminated weapons complex is put at over $200 billion.

• On the outskirts of Paris, 2,500 concrete barrels were found to have leaked plutonium into the soil near a children's playground.

• A study by Greenpeace revealed that there were 3,200 accidents involving nuclear navies in the 1980's.

• Medical research in the UK found strong evidence of a link between leukemia in children and fathers who worked at the Sellafield nuclear reprocessing plant.

• Typhoons in the 1980's swept into the Pacific Ocean huge amounts of nuclear waste, including plutonium, resulting from over 100 French nuclear tests on the tiny islands of Polynesia.

• At the US Rocky Flats nuclear plant, 62 pounds of plutonium, enough to make seven nuclear bombs, were found lodged in air ducts.

• In 1990 a US Government trust fund of $100 million was established to compensate people injured by unsafe operation of nuclear weapons plants.

Proliferation in the Third World

With clear evidence of the rush by the major powers to build up enormous stocks of high-tech and mass destruction weapons, it is not surprising that the fever was catching. To those Third World countries not charter members of the club but with their own interests in national prestige, deterring enemies, and/or overpowering their neighbors, weapons of mass destruction have attractive features: they are seen as the unchallenged status symbols of military power and, in view of their role in keeping the peace between the superpowers for 45 years, as a practical means of discouraging attack.

Nuclear weapons might have been the first choice for many countries, but these weapons require advanced technology, a tremendous investment of resources, and a good deal of time. A number of developing countries nevertheless have tried the nuclear route, a few successfully, all secretly. India first tested a nuclear device in 1974 and since then may have produced a modest arsenal, including low-yield atom bombs and a warhead for a missile. Its neighbor, Pakistan, responded with an aggressive development program which has given it the capability to produce a bomb quickly, if it has not already done so. With Israel as partner, South Africa is also thought to have developed a small arsenal. Argentina and Brazil have both had secret programs but in 1990, under civilian presidents, agreed to cease their activities and open the facilities to joint inspection. In addition, North Korea, Iran, Iraq, and Taiwan are said to be trying, but are still some years from actually producing nuclear weapons.

Chemical weapons (CW), offering less formidable technological problems than nuclear, have been the alternative choice for many developing countries. CW are cheaper and apparently easier to acquire or produce, although neither cheap nor easy to defend against—nor dispose of. As instruments of mass destruction, they are by no means as effective as nuclear bombs, but used against an unprotected population they can be powerful weapons of terror. To the nuclear have-nots, therefore, they are viewed as appropriate and affordable deterrents to nuclear as well as conventional attack.

Unlike nuclear, the use of CW is outlawed by international treaty (page 44), but there is no prohibition as yet on production or possession.

The international ban on use appears to have been relatively effective over the 65 years since it was signed. There have been exceptions, however, and a blatant one recently was Iraq's CW attacks on Iran in the 1980–88 war. This well-documented use, which produced no official outcry of international condemnation, is one reason for concern that it has eroded constraint and helped to stimulate the race for chemical arms. Allegations of use, some more convincing than others, have also been made in recent years against: Burma, Ethiopia, the Philippines, and Sudan (in all four cases, of use by government forces against rebels within the country), also Egypt (in its intervention in Yemen in the 1960's), South Africa (in Angola), Thailand (in Laos and Cambodia), and Vietnam (in Cambodia).

Developing countries which are on current lists of likely possessors of chemical weapons include: Burma, China,

*Early in the Gulf War the coalition forces claimed that they had destroyed Iraq's nuclear, chemical, and biological facilities. Later uncertainties led the allies to include destruction of these weapons as one requirement of the peace agreement.

CHART 9

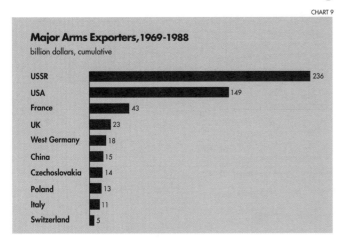

Major Arms Exporters, 1969-1988
billion dollars, cumulative

USSR	236
USA	149
France	43
UK	23
West Germany	18
China	15
Czechoslovakia	14
Poland	13
Italy	11
Switzerland	5

The international traffic in conventional arms is a profitable and thriving business. In the 20 years ending in 1988, 66 countries shipped arms abroad, with an estimated value of $588 billion. The ten countries shown on *chart 9* exported 89 percent of this total, with the two superpowers alone accounting for 65 percent of it. Included in the deliveries to developing countries were 49,524 tactical guided missiles, half of which went to the Middle East.

Major Arms Importers in the Third World 1969–1988
billion dollars, cumulative

Country	Value	Country	Value
Iraq	61.1	Afghanistan	10.2
Saudi Arabia	37.2	Algeria	9.8
Vietnam	29.0	Ethiopia	9.3
Syria	27.9	Taiwan	8.1
Libya	26.6	S. Korea	7.6
Iran	26.0	Turkey	7.0
India	21.7	Jordan	6.2
Cuba	16.3	Greece	5.9
Egypt	15.8	Pakistan	5.1
Angola	11.3	S. Yemen	4.9

The biggest market for arms is the Third World, and the most lucrative region of all is the Middle East. Of the top 10 arms importers in the 20 years 1969–1988, five countries were in the Middle East, which was soon to explode into war. Of the top 20 importers, 13 countries had governments noted for the frequent use of violence, including torture and brutality, against their own people; 15 of the countries were under military-controlled governments (pp. 18–19).

Egypt, India, Iran, Iraq, N. Korea, S. Korea, Libya, Syria, Taiwan, Pakistan, and Vietnam. It should be emphasized, however, that all such lists on this subject have a high degree of uncertainty. As far as chemical weapons go, tight official secrecy is generally the rule, which means that allegations and accusations are more available than facts. On one point, however, observers seem to be agreed, and that is that the number of Third World countries acquiring or trying to acquire a CW capability has sharply increased. Meanwhile, actions to curb the spread of these weapons by controlling exports continue in the developed countries, and negotiations for a formal global treaty banning them entirely are underway in Geneva.

Biological weapons (BW) are also on the international agenda in terms of concern and control. Although BW are under full prohibition by treaty, US intelligence has continued to make allegations of violations by a number of countries, including the USSR and Iraq. No public evidence has been presented. Questioned on this subject about Iraq last year, the Director of CIA said that it was not so important because the size of Iraq's chemical capability meant that "they can do [with it] substantially everything they can do with BW capability."

Chemical Weapons in Developed Countries

Since the summary above addresses the situation in the Third World only, it should be noted that substantial stocks of chemical weapons are known to exist in developed countries. The US and USSR both have inventories of grotesque size (tens of thousands of tons each) which they plan to reduce to 5,000 tons each by the year 2002. France in 1988 announced a production program but subsequently stated formally that it had no chemical weapons. Israel, though officially secret about its CW, is alleged to have stocks for offensive use and is the one country with a significant program for population protection, which it repeatedly used in defense against the Iraqi Scud missile attacks of early 1991.

Other countries which may still have CW stocks from World War II, but are destroying them, or plan to, are: Australia, Belgium, Canada, Denmark, and Italy. NATO stocks in Germany are to be removed by the US before 1992. The destruction of CW stocks is proving a major headache for all countries. Costs are substantial, as are technical and environmental problems.

Ballistic missiles add another dimension to the proliferation of unconventional weapons. Since long-range missiles may carry nuclear, chemical, and even biological payloads, the combination is believed to enlarge the danger that warheads of mass destruction will be used. The recent proliferation of missile programs includes increases in the number of countries possessing them, the number modifying or producing them, and the power and range of missiles in the arsenals. Based on information available:

• More than a dozen developing countries now have missiles in service; about half of those are also believed to have CW, and two have nuclear weapons.

• CIA has forecast that, by the year 2000, at least 15 developing countries will be producing their own missiles.

• The range of Third World missiles is stretching out. Most have a range of under 200 miles, but Iraq successfully modernized a Scud missile from 190 to 375 miles; India has under development the Aqui to go 1,550 miles; and Saudi Arabia received from China the CSS-2 with a range of 1,600–1,800 miles.

The race for the most advanced military technology began in the highly industrialized countries, and for a while it was confined there. It is now rapidly spreading in the Third World, largely with assistance both in equipment and technical aid of the military-industrial complex in the developed countries. But there is increasing effort by the developing to establish independent, indigenous capabilities. In time more of them will.

The prospects make clear that the machinery of control so far available has not put a serious brake on the spread of the most dangerous and destabilizing weapons ever designed. One good reason may be that the major powers have failed to demonstrate the self-restraint that might serve as a model. Another factor is that, once started in a region, the competition has a ripple effect which steadily spreads. It is unlikely to stop until there is a change of priorities not only for others but for ourselves. Perhaps this will be seen as a more urgent need as unrestrained technology extends the reach of weapons from the Third World into the centers of power of the industrial world.

MAP 2

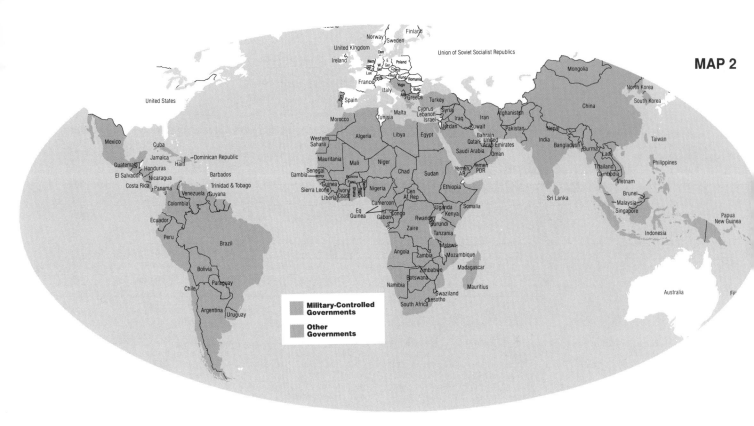

Military Control and Repression in the Third World

Military-Controlled Governments

Region and Country	1989-90 Official Violence Against the Public	1989 Armed Forces per 1,000 population	1960-90 Years of Military Rule	Years at War	Deaths in Wars (1,000)
Latin America					
Argentina	none	3.5	17	5	16
Brazil	frequent	2.2	24	1	1
Chile	frequent	7.4	18	3	28
Colombia	frequent	4.4	10	8	86
El Salvador	frequent	10.7	14	12	75
Guatemala	frequent	4.8	27	25	140
Haiti	some	1.1	20	—	—
Honduras	some	3.6	27	<1	5
Panama	some	5.1	23	1	1
Paraguay	some	3.8	31	<1	—
Peru	some	5.5	22	8	17
Europe					
Turkey	frequent	11.9	31	4	5
Middle East					
Cyprus	none	14.4	17	1	5
Egypt	frequent	8.5	—	4	75
Iran	frequent	9.2	31	21	588
Iraq	frequent	54.7	31	11	115
Jordan	some	20.7	31	<1	10
Kuwait	some	9.9	<1	—	—
Lebanon	some	7.2	16	11	163
Syria	frequent	33.5	28	<1	20
Yemen, AR	some	4.9	29	8	15
South Asia					
Afghanistan	frequent	3.7	18	12	1,300
Bangladesh	frequent	.9	14	<1	1,000
Pakistan	some	4.6	27	5	9
Sri Lanka	frequent	1.3	3	8	40
Far East					
Burma	frequent	5.6	29	5	14
Cambodia	some	6.2	24	22	1,221
Indonesia	some	1.6	25	11	660
Korea, N.	some	49.6	31	—	—
Korea, S.	some	17.4	30	<1	1
Laos	frequent	13.8	29	14	30
Taiwan	some	18.3	31	—	—
Thailand	some	5.2	28	—	—
Vietnam	frequent	16.0	31	19	2,394
Oceania					
Fiji	none	6.8	4	—	—
Africa					
Algeria	some	5.1	26	5	35
Angola	frequent	10.3	12	31	396
Benin	some	.9	28	—	—
Burk. Faso	some	1.0	25	—	—
Burundi	some	1.3	25	2	115
Cen. Afr. R.	some	2.1	25	—	—
Chad	frequent	3.1	16	8	7
Congo	some	4.6	23	—	—
Eq. Guinea	some	2.3	22	—	—
Ethiopia	frequent	7.0	17	25	609
Ghana	none	.8	20	<1	1
Guinea	some	1.5	7	—	—
Lesotho	some	1.2	5	—	—
Liberia	frequent	3.2	11	2	11
Libya	some	19.4	22	—	—
Malawi	some	.9	5	—	—
Mali	some	.8	23	—	—
Mauritania	some	5.6	13	—	—
Mozambique	frequent	2.6	13	21	1,080
Niger	some	.4	17	—	—
Nigeria	some	.9	7	7	2,006
Rwanda	some	.7	18	6	63
Sierra Leone	some	.7	4	—	—
Somalia	frequent	8.7	22	3	55
S. Africa	frequent	3.0	5	8	10
Sudan	frequent	3.1	25	17	1,006
Togo	some	1.8	24	—	—
Uganda	frequent	2.0	22	18	613
Zaire	frequent	1.5	26	6	100

Other Third-World Governments

Region and Country	1989-90 Official Violence Against the Public	1989 Armed Forces per 1,000 population	1960-90 Years of Military Rule	Years at War	Deaths in Wars (1,000)
Latin America					
Barbados	none	—	—	—	—
Bolivia	some	3.9	14	—	—
Costa Rica	none	—	—	—	—
Cuba	some	17.6	17	—	—
Domin. Rep.	none	3.3	4	1	3
Ecuador	some	5.5	15	—	—
Guyana	none	2.0	—	—	—
Jamaica	none	1.2	—	1	1
Mexico	none	1.7	—	—	—
Nicaragua	frequent	17.1	29	10	80
Trin. & Tob.	none	2.4	—	—	—
Uruguay	some	8.1	8	—	—
Venezuela	none	3.7	—	—	—
Europe					
Albania	frequent	15.0	—	—	—
Greece	some	16.1	6	—	—
Malta	none	2.9	—	—	—
Portugal	some	6.6	2	—	—
Yugoslavia	some	7.6	—	—	—
Middle East					
Bahrain	frequent	12.0	—	—	—
Oman	none	21.1	—	—	—
Qatar	none	22.6	—	—	—
Saudi Arabia	some	5.0	—	—	—
UAE	none	28.5	—	—	—
Yemen, PDR	some	11.6	—	2	11
South Asia					
India	frequent	1.5	—	11	49
Nepal	some	1.9	—	—	—
Far East					
Brunei	none	15.5	—	—	—
China	some	2.8	—	5	506
Malaysia	some	7.7	—	1	1
Mongolia	some	10.2	—	—	—
Philippines	frequent	1.8	—	36	75
Singapore	some	20.9	—	—	—
Oceania					
Papua NG	none	1.0	—	—	—
Africa					
Botswana	none	3.2	—	—	—
Cameroon	some	1.1	—	1	5
Gabon	some	4.4	—	—	—
Gambia	some	1.2	—	—	—
Ivory C.	some	.6	—	—	—
Kenya	some	1.0	—	4	5
Madagascar	some	1.8	—	—	—
Mauritius	...	...	—	—	—
Morocco	frequent	7.8	—	—	—
Namibia	...	...	—	—	—
Senegal	some	1.4	—	—	—
Swaziland	...	...	—	—	—
Tanzania	some	1.8	—	—	—
Tunisia	some	4.8	—	—	—
Zambia	some	2.0	—	1	1
Zimbabwe	some	5.8	—	11	16

— none or negligible   . . . not available   <1 less than one year at war

Criteria for Classifications

Official Violence Against the Public
- ■ frequent
- ▨ some
- □ none

Military control

Key political leadership by military officers; existence of a state of emergency or martial law; extrajudicial authority exercised by security forces; lack of central political control over armed forces; occupation by foreign military forces.

Official violence against the public

Torture, brutality, disappearances, and political killings. Gradations of "none," "some," "frequent" reflect available evidence of frequency of government use of repression in the most extreme form.

Military-Controlled compared with Other Governments

	1989-90 Official Violence Against the Public ■ ▨ □ # of countries			1989 Armed Forces per 1,000 pop.	1960-90 Military Rule av. # of yrs.	Years At War av. # of yrs.	Deaths in Wars 1,000
Military-Controlled	32	27	5	6.4	20.0	6.0	14,141
Other Third World	9	25	15	2.6	1.9	1.7	753

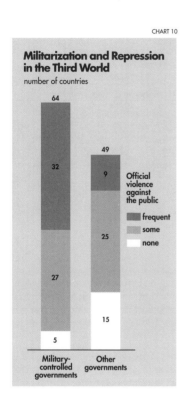

CHART 10

Militarization and Repression in the Third World

number of countries

64

49

32

9

Official violence against the public

■ frequent

■ some

□ none

27

25

5

15

Military-controlled governments

Other governments

Militarized Political Power

Despite the quantity of sophisticated military equipment flooding into the Third World, the armed forces in these countries remain very large. In other words, the concept that firepower would substitute for manpower has not yet taken hold. While the armed forces in the developed countries have stabilized, in the developing countries their numbers have continued to grow, and currently are about twice as large as they were in 1960. The build-up of forces, the growth of military expenditures, and the investment in arms imports have all proceeded at a faster pace in the Third World than in the industrialized.

One result of these trends is that the military forces have established an influential political base throughout the developing world. They represent the largest single element in most government bureaucracies, the largest financial resources and, of course, the power of the sword. They also have several other unique advantages. They provide the visible trappings of prestige for political leaders, civilian or military: the requisite honor guards, jet aircraft, helicopters. They have a direct line to the world of wealth and business, the arms-producing corporations that are both beneficiaries of government largesse and contributors to political power. And they deal in matters of national security which can, to an extent largely within their own control, be made secret and inaccessible both to the public and to any of the usual checks and balances within the government.

All of these factors would help to ensure the political influence of the armed forces under normal conditions. The de-colonization* of the past three decades, however, provided exceptional opportunities for entree into the political field. Where there was limited experience in self-government and administration, the military came to represent the strongest sources of leadership. In 1960, 26 percent of the developing states that were then independent were under military domination in some form. By 1989–90, the proportion was up to 57 percent; that is, in 64 of the 113 countries included in this study armed forces, domestic and foreign, exercised significant executive, judicial, and/or legislative power (see *criteria,* page opposite).

Countries in which the military play a political role have several features in common. They tend to be more heavily militarized: that is, their military expenditures per capita and their men under arms relative to population average twice as high as in other Third World countries. As the summary table opposite indicates, the currently militarized governments also have a history of military control. On average, the military have exercised political power for 20 of the past 30 years, in comparison with an average of 2 years in the other governments. In addition, these countries under military control have suffered more wars: three times as many as in the rest of the Third World; and an incredible number of deaths in wars, a total of 14,141,000 deaths since 1960, 19 times as many as in the other Third World countries.

Aside from the connection between militarized political control and the frequency of war, there is also a disturbing pattern of official violence within the countries that are under military-dominated governments. Of the 64 countries so identified in the map and table opposite, 59 of them have used force and repression against the public. Half have made frequent use of force in the form of torture, brutality, disappearances, or political killings. The human rights records of other Third World governments are by no means universally favorable, but the use of violence against the people is much less common.

Despite their shocking record on human rights, none of the countries which frequently practised extreme forms of repression failed to receive a substantial flow of arms from obliging suppliers. In the most recent reporting period, 1984–88, 56 percent of the arms delivered to the Third World went to countries with highly repressive governments. The largest supplier, according to US official estimates, was the USSR (especially to Iraq, India, Syria, Afghanistan, and Angola); the next in rank were US and France, both of which supplied arms to a larger number of repressive regimes but in smaller quantities.

* 52 of the 113 developing countries in this report became independent after 1959.

MAP 3

The Killing Fields
1500 to 1990

- over 10,000,000 deaths
- over 1,000,000 deaths
- 1,000 to 1,000,000 deaths
- no wars

Battlefields of 1990[1]

Angola	Liberia
Colombia	Mozambique
El Salvador	Peru
Ethiopia	Somalia
Guatemala	South Africa
India	Sri Lanka
Kuwait	Sudan
Lebanon	Tibet

[1] Wars with annual deaths of 1,000 or more.

Warfare's Toll

There are some fortunate countries in the map above, but not very many. Of the 142 countries covered in this survey, only 32 have had no war on their soil—no war since 1500, when William Eckhardt begins his record of wars and their attendant tragedies. The lucky few countries which have escaped war so far are, for the most part, relatively new (independent only since the 1960's or later) or very small (under 500,000 population).

The rest of the world in this period has lived through 589 wars and lost 141,901,000 lives to them. The trend by century, as shown in *chart 11*, is far from encouraging. Beginning with the 17th, every century has registered an increase in the number of wars and in the number of deaths associated with them. The rise in war deaths has far outstripped the rise in population. The 20th century in particular has been a stand-out in the history of warfare. Wars now are shockingly more destructive and deadly. So far, in the 90 years of this century, there have been over four times as many war deaths as in the 400 years preceding.

As for the geography of war, the historical record points to Europe as the principal locale by far—site of two world wars and of two-thirds of all war deaths since 1500. Since World War II, however, Europe has dropped to last place in regional comparisons, and the Far East has moved to the top, accounting for more than half of the war dead since 1945. Without exception, the wars of the last two decades have all been in the developing world.

Two aspects of the recent war record call for special mention:

The first should arouse citizens to demand a place in the decision-making process before a war can begin. For the evidence is that civilians are now by far the main victims in wars. In this century many more unarmed civilians than professional soldiers have died in wars. In the decade of the 1980's, the proportion of civilian deaths jumped to 74 percent of the total and in 1990 it appears to have been close to 90 percent.

The second is for government policy-makers to ponder. In earlier centuries the aggressor seemed to have a 50-50 change of winning the war, but this no longer holds. The changes of the starter of a war being victorious are shrinking. In the 1980's only 18 percent of the starters were winners.

There is, unfortunately, no adequate historical record of the global costs of wars going beyond the count of war-related casualties or deaths. Even official budgetary outlays are available only for some wars. Of one thing we can be sure, however, and that is that the costs that show up in military budgets represent only a small fraction of the price society has paid and will pay for its failure to find non-military alternatives to war. None of the major alternatives—eg. embargo, arms control, diplomacy—has yet been given a full and fair trail.

"We should use up all possibilities for a political solution before force."
Yevgeny M. Primakov
USSR, 1990

CHART 11

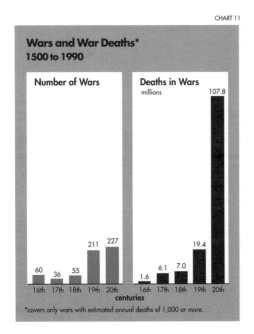

Wars and War Deaths*
1500 to 1990

Number of Wars	Deaths in Wars

*covers only wars with estimated annual deaths of 1,000 or more.

In some respects, it was like many other wars.

Like 30 other international wars since World War II, the Persian Gulf War began with an invasion.

The invader, Iraq, was militarily more powerful than the country invaded, Kuwait.

The United States took military action without a clear statement of objectives for the American public.

The United Nations demanded that the aggressor withdraw. Iraq did not.

In some countries, the war proved to be a welcome reprieve from economic and social problems at home.

The war was a testing ground for the latest in high-tech weapons and aircraft.

Both sides controlled the media and used them for tactical military advantage.

The enemy was made larger than life and more devilish than Satan.

It was a military victory but a human disaster, in terms of bloodshed, destruction, floods of refugees, unsolved political problems.

The country starting the war was defeated.

In other respects, the Persian Gulf War was unique.

The day after the invasion, the US ordered naval forces and combat troops to the Gulf.

The international response to the invasion was the very model of collective action.

The UN embargoed all trade with Iraq except medicine and some food; the embargo was a success.

The US served as organizer and fund raiser of a coalition of 37 countries to repel the aggressor.

With arms budgets over 50 times as large as Iraq's, the allies represented an unusual array of power against a single nation.

The allies attacked with the most deadly air assault on record.

It was the first made-for-TV war, with smart bombs and stealth fighters on display.

After five weeks of 88,000 air sorties by the allies, the ground war against Iraq lasted only 100 hours.

When it was over, a major US newspaper described it as the greatest mismatch in modern warfare.

The victorious general said the campaign was unique in the annals of military history.

Paying the Piper for the Persian Gulf War

With a brief but major war just concluded as this is written (early March 1991), it may be an appropriate time for a quick run-through of the range of costs, both immediate and long-term, that a war like this inevitably levies, even though they cannot all be totted up in dollars.

Military budgets—For the US, which was by far the major contributor of forces to the coalition against Iraq, incremental costs of the Gulf War since August 1990 are currently estimated at about $48 billion, with possibly another $12 billion in wind-up costs. A total of $60 billion is in itself a relatively modest sum against a Department of Defense annual budget five times as large. Several other factors, largely unique to this war, make it appear even more of a bargain for US taxpayers:

• Allies have pledged $53 billion to defray US costs.

• This is officially an off-budget war, meaning that it will not come under US budget restrictions, nor affect other expenditures.

• No war tax is planned to burden today's taxpayers.

Veterans and interest—All participants in a war also face longer-term costs which are unlikely to appear in military budgets. Typical are medical and pension costs for wounded and other veterans. Recent research by the Institute for Policy Studies (IPS) suggests that these costs go on for years and, in the US at least, tend to be almost three times the original outlays for a war.

Governments like the US which are already suffering large budget deficits, will have to borrow to finance these costs. Over several decades, IPS calculates, interest rates could more than double all costs previously mentioned. In short, for the US alone, assuming that about two-thirds of the allies' pledges will be paid soon, the charges against the budget are likely to be closer to $160 than $60 billion. Without the allies' help, they could mount to $400 billion, and that is in the prices of today. Of course most of this war's debt will be paid by our children and grandchildren and at the much higher prices of the future.

Social and economic costs—Beyond official budget expenditures are the broader losses to society resulting from wartime disruptions and destruction. In the Gulf War, these included: the deaths of 50,000 or more civilians; the loss of hundreds of thousands of jobs in Kuwait by foreign workers (in Pakistan alone, $2 billion in wage remittances lost); the drop in international travel, estimated at 30 percent by US airlines; the losses in trade and tourism, (by Turkey alone, $9 billion) and, to top it all, over 500 Kuwaiti oil wells burning and vast material destruction in the war zone. Rehabilitation in Kuwait is estimated to cost $70 billion in 1991 dollars; in Iraq, perhaps $200 billion.

The ramifications are very broad. Recovery assistance going to the front-line states is likely to slow development aid for others in the Third World; the rise in oil prices has intensified the adjustment problems in Eastern Europe; pollution from the burning oil fields may reduce crop yields as far away as India. In fact, the war has ravaged the environment, threatening global climate and, in the heavily bombed areas, potentially catastrophic effects on the public's health.

Political costs—Like many wars, this one has left in its wake unstable and possibly long-lasting political effects. While it is too early to see signposts of what is ahead, a few of the uncertainties can be identified:

• Postwar insurrections, with neighboring states aiding Kurds in the north and Shiites in the south, threaten the integrity of Iraq.

• One more defeat has stirred new tensions in the Arab world and may open a debate on democracy (including the rights of women), which could affect not only Hussein of Iraq but other Arab leaders as well.

• The wartime hiatus in important European disarmament negotiations may have strengthened the influence of hardliners in both the USSR and US, restricting progress.

• In giving the war legitimacy, the UN—and the US as initiator—may have lost stature among those critical of the conduct of the war and the catastrophic damage.

• The lead role of the US in prosecuting the war leaves it with major responsibility for effective action on the many unresolved problems of the region, including the Israeli-Palestinian conflict.

Those are the kinds of uncertainties even a "successful" war leaves with us. Will the longer-term results be favorable and warrant the sacrifice of so many lives and the loss of so much wealth? Or will the war be a stimulus for a further arms buildup, sharpening the appetite for high-tech weapons and serving as a model for the use of military force to resolve political disputes?

Wars and War-Related Deaths, 1500–1990

Location and Identification of Conflict[1]	Number of Deaths Civilian	Military	Total
North America	**204,000**	**1,288,000**	**1,532,000**
Canada			94,000
1914–18 World War I	0	55,000	55,000
1939–45 World War II	0	39,000	39,000
United States			1,438,000
1637–37 US vs Pequot Indians	1,000	0	1,000
1763–63 Indians vs UK	…	…	1,000
1778–83 US revolt UK (3 Eu interv.)	…	34,000	34,000
1812–15 War of 1812, US vs UK	…	5,000	5,000
1813–14 Creek Indians vs Whites	1,000	0	1,000
1835–36 Texas vs Mexico	1,000	1,000	2,000
1861–65 Confederacy vs Government	200,000	620,000	820,000
1861–80 Conquest of the West; massacres	…	…	33,000
1861–67 US vs Sioux Indians	…	…	6,000
1876–77 Sioux Indians vs US	1,000	0	1,000
1917–18 World War I	0	126,000	126,000
1941–45 World War II	0	408,000	408,000
Latin America	**1,932,000**	**1,088,000**	**3,239,000**
Argentina			39,000
1833–34 Indian uprising	…	…	1,000
1841–51 Libs v Govt; UK, Fr invad.	10,000	1,000	11,000
1851–52 Libs vs Gov; Brazil interv.	…	1,000	1,000
1863–63 Montoneros vs Government	…	…	1,000
1866–67 Federalists vs Government	…	…	1,000
1870–71 Province vs Government	…	…	2,000
1874–75 Buenos Aires v Government	…	…	1,000
1880–80 Buenos Aires v Government	…	…	1,000
1955–55 Armed forces vs Peron	2,000	2,000	4,000
1976–79 "Disappearances"	12,000	3,000	15,000
1982–82 Arg vs UK in Falklands	0	1,000	1,000
Bolivia			203,000
1841–41 Peru vs Bolivia	…	1,000	1,000
1932–35 Paraguay vs Bol. (Chaco War)	70,000	130,000	200,000
1952–52 Revolution vs Govt	1,000	1,000	2,000
Brazil			1,110,000
1657–61 Netherlands vs Portugal	…	4,000	4,000
1864–70 Para vs Brazil & Argentina	800,000	300,000	1,100,000
1893–94 Conservatives vs Govt	…	…	2,000
1896–97 Canudos vs Government	…	…	1,000
1932–32 State vs Federal Govt	…	…	1,000
1944–45 World War II; troops in Italy	0	1,000	1,000
1980–80 Rightist terrorism	…	…	1,000
Chile			36,000
1851–51 Liberals vs Government	…	…	3,000
1891–91 Congress vs Government	…	…	5,000
1973–73 Military coup; US interv.	…	…	5,000
1974–74 Executions by Govt	20,000	0	20,000
1987–87 Mine strikers vs Army	3,000	0	3,000
Colombia			563,000
1840–42 Liberals vs Government	…	…	4,000
1854–54 Democrats vs Dictator	…	…	1,000
1860–62 Liberals vs Government	…	…	3,000
1876–77 Conservatives vs Govt	…	…	1,000
1879–79 Massacre revolutionaries	…	…	80,000
1884–85 Liberals vs Government	…	…	1,000
1899–03 Liberals vs Government	75,000	75,000	150,000
1948–48 Conservatives vs Govt	…	…	1,000
1949–62 Liberals vs Government	200,000	100,000	300,000
1986–90 Civilians killed by Govt	14,000	8,000	22,000
Costa Rica			2,000
1948–48 Natl Un. vs Govt; US interv.	1,000	1,000	2,000
Cuba			485,000
1868–78 Cuba vs Spain	75,000	75,000	150,000
1895–98 Cuba vs Spain; US interv.	80,000	50,000	130,000
1898–98 US vs Spain over Cuba & Phil	190,000	10,000	200,000
1958–59 Castro vs Batista; US interv.	2,000	3,000	5,000
Dominican Republic			15,000
1863–65 Spain vs Santo Domingo	…	7,000	7,000
1937–37 Haitians in DR massacred	5,000	0	5,000
1965–65 US intervene in civil war	1,000	2,000	3,000
Ecuador			1,000
1863–63 Colombia vs Ecuador	0	1,000	1,000
El Salvador			109,000
1885–85 Guatemala vs El Salvador	…	1,000	1,000
1906–06 Guat vs El Sal & Honduras	0	1,000	1,000
1931–32 Peasant uprising & mass	24,000	8,000	32,000
1979–90 Dem. Sal. Front vs Govt	50,000	25,000	75,000
Guatemala			141,000
1954–54 Conserv. vs Govt; US interv.	…	…	1,000
1966–90 Govt mass Indians; US interv.	100,000	40,000	140,000
Haiti			20,000
1802–03 Haiti vs France	12,000	8,000	20,000
Honduras			7,000
1907–07 Nic vs El Sal & Honduras	0	1,000	1,000
1924–24 Conservatives vs Govt	…	…	1,000
1969–69 El Sal vs Hond (Soccer War)	3,000	2,000	5,000
Jamaica			1,000
1980–80 Election violence	1,000	0	1,000
Mexico			316,000
1520–21 Spain conquered Mexico	…	…	2,000
1829–29 Mexican revolt vs Spain	1,000	0	1,000
1832–32 Liberals vs Government	…	…	4,000
1846–48 US vs Mexico	4,000	17,000	21,000
1858–61 Lib v Govt; UK, Fr, Sp, Aus interv.	…	…	8,000
1862–67 Fr vs Juarez; A–H interv.	…	20,000	20,000
1910–20 Lib & Rad vs Govt; US interv.	125,000	125,000	250,000
1926–30 Con Cristeros vs Govt	…	…	10,000

Location and Identification of Conflict[1]	Number of Deaths Civilian	Military	Total
Nicaragua			82,000
1855–57 Liberals vs Government	…	…	2,000
1978–79 Sandinistas vs Somoza	25,000	25,000	50,000
1981–88 Contras vs Sandinistas	15,000	15,000	30,000
Panama			1,000
1989–89 US invaded Panama	1,000	0	1,000
Paraguay			3,000
1911–12 Liberals vs Government	…	…	2,000
1947–47 Liberals vs Government	…	…	1,000
Peru			44,000
1531–31 Spain conquered Peru	1,000	0	1,000
1853–58 Liberals vs Conservatives	…	…	7,000
1865–66 Sp vs Chil & Per; Bol, Ecua interv.	0	1,000	1,000
1879–83 Chile vs Peru & Bolivia	…	14,000	14,000
1894–95 Liberals vs Government	…	…	4,000
1983–90 Shining Path vs Govt	9,000	8,000	17,000
Uruguay			1,000
1903–04 Conservatives vs Govt	…	…	1,000
Venezuela			23,000
1859–63 Liberals vs Government	…	…	20,000
1868–71 Conservatives vs Govt	…	…	3,000
Latin America (area-wide)			37,000
1810–25 Independence from Spain[2]	…	…	37,000
Europe	**48,935,000**	**44,119,000**	**93,450,000**
Albania			35,000
1830–31 Albanians vs Turkey	4,000	1,000	5,000
1941–44 World War II	10,000	20,000	30,000
Austria			3,640,000
1520–33 Turkey vs Austro-Hungary	15,000	85,000	100,000
1739–48 Prussia invaded Austria	…	359,000	359,000
1778–79 Prussia invade Austria	…	2,000	2,000
1848–48 Liberals vs Government	…	…	4,000
1848–49 Sardinia vs Austria-Hung.	2,000	9,000	11,000
1866–66 Prus & It vs Aust; Fr interv.	100,000	50,000	150,000
1878–78 Bosnian rebellion vs A-H	2,000	4,000	6,000
1881–81 Dalmatians vs Aust-Hung	1,000	0	1,000
1914–18 World War I (incl. Hungary)	300,000	2,300,000	2,600,000
1934–34 Socialists vs Fascist Govt	1,000	1,000	2,000
1939–45 World War II	125,000	280,000	405,000
Balkans			274,000
1716–18 Austria vs Turkey	…	16,000	16,000
1736–39 Russia & Austria vs Turkey	…	38,000	38,000
1768–74 Russia vs Turkey	…	28,000	28,000
1787–92 Russia vs Turkey (Aust interv.)	…	192,000	192,000
Belgium			321,000
1830–33 Belg vs Neth; UK, Fr invad.	…	…	3,000
1914–18 World War I	30,000	88,000	118,000
1940–40 World War II	90,000	110,000	200,000
Bulgaria			370,000
1875–77 Balkan rebellion vs Turkey	20,000	10,000	30,000
1885–85 Serb vs Bulgar; A-H interv.	1,000	2,000	3,000
1915–18 World War I	275,000	28,000	303,000
1941–45 World War II (Allied 1944–45)	14,000	20,000	34,000
Crete			72,000
1645–69 Turk vs Venice over Crete	…	72,000	72,000
Czechoslovakia			280,000
1939–45 World War II	250,000	30,000	280,000
Denmark			11,000
1848–49 Prussia vs Denmark	…	6,000	6,000
1864–64 Prussia & A-H vs Denmark	…	5,000	5,000
Estonia			22,000
1600–04 Sweden vs Poland	…	22,000	22,000
Finland			173,000
1788–90 Russia vs Swed (Denmk interv.)	…	3,000	3,000
1918–18 Communists vs Govt	…	…	20,000
1939–40 USSR vs Finland	…	90,000	90,000
1941–44 World War II	15,000	45,000	60,000
France			4,741,000
1544–46 England vs France	…	8,000	8,000
1550–56 France vs Spain	…	95,000	95,000
1557–60 France vs Haps (UK interv.)	…	11,000	11,000
1562–64 Huguenot vs France; UK interv.	8,000	6,000	14,000
1567–68 Huguenot vs France	5,000	3,000	8,000
1569–70 Huguenot vs France	11,000	9,000	20,000
1572–73 France vs Huguenot	50,000	2,000	52,000
1575–76 Huguenot vs France	2,000	1,000	3,000
1585–89 Huguenot vs France	…	4,000	4,000
1590–98 France vs Spain	…	17,000	17,000
1650–59 Spain vs France	…	108,000	108,000
1656–59 UK & France vs Spain	…	15,000	15,000
1702–06 "Camisard" Insurrection	…	4,000	4,000
1792–02 French Revolutionary Wars	1,000,000	1,030,000	2,030,000
1830–30 Liberals vs Government	…	…	2,000
1831–35 Political Troubles	…	…	6,000
1848–48 Liberals vs Government	…	…	3,000
1851–51 Royalists vs Government	…	…	1,000
1871–71 Natl Guard vs Govt; Ger interv.	…	…	20,000
1914–18 World War I	40,000	1,630,000	1,670,000
1939–45 World War II (Allied 39–40, 44–45)	450,000	200,000	650,000
Germany			13,815,000
1524–25 Peasants' War	100,000	75,000	175,000
1546–47 Protestants vs Holy Rom Emp.	…	8,000	8,000
1618–48 France & Sweden vs HRE	2,000,000	2,000,000	4,000,000
1870–71 France vs Germany/Prussia	62,000	188,000	250,000
1914–18 World War I	760,000	2,400,000	3,160,000
1934–34 Socialists vs Nazi Govt	1,000	0	1,000
1939–45 World War II	1,471,000	4,750,000	6,221,000

William Eckhardt, Research Director of the Lentz Peace Research Laboratory, prepares the war data for this publication.

See page 25 for definitions and footnotes.

Wars and War-Related Deaths, 1500–1990

Location and Identification of Conflict[1]		Number of Deaths Civilian	Military	Total
Greece				**482,000**
1821–28	Greek rev. Turk; UK interv.	105,000	15,000	120,000
1857–58	Greek mutiny vs UK & France	...	1,000	1,000
1917–18	World War I	132,000	5,000	137,000
1940–41	World War II	54,000	10,000	64,000
1945–49	UK intervenes in civil war	...	...	160,000
Hungary				**1,600,000**
1537–41	Austria-Hungary vs Turkey	...	51,000	51,000
1566–68	Turkey vs Austria-Hungary	...	24,000	24,000
1590–96	Austria vs Turkey	...	40,000	40,000
1593–06	Turkey vs Austria-Hungary	...	90,000	90,000
1657–57	Hungary vs Turkey	...	...	1,000
1663–64	Turkey vs Austria-Hungary	...	20,000	20,000
1682–99	Turkey vs Austria & Poland	...	384,000	384,000
1703–11	Hungarian Revolt vs Aust	...	43,000	43,000
1711–11	Turkey vs Russia in Hung	...	2,000	2,000
1848–49	Hungary vs A-H & Russia	...	60,000	60,000
1919–19	Czech & Romania vs Hung	...	11,000	11,000
1919–20	Anti-Communists vs Govt	...	...	4,000
1941–45	World War II	450,000	400,000	850,000
1956–56	USSR intervenes in civ war	10,000	10,000	20,000
Italy				**1,592,000**
1499–03	Turkey vs Venice	...	4,000	4,000
1501–04	France vs Spain for Naples	...	20,000	20,000
1508–09	Cambrian League vs Venice	...	10,000	10,000
1512–14	Holy League vs France	...	25,000	25,000
1515–16	France vs Swiss for Milan	...	4,000	4,000
1521–26	France vs Spain	...	31,000	31,000
1526–29	France vs Spain	...	18,000	18,000
1535–37	France vs Spain	...	75,000	75,000
1542–45	France & Turkey vs Spain	...	77,000	77,000
1556–59	France vs Spain & UK	...	24,000	24,000
1570–71	Turkey vs Venice	...	38,000	38,000
1701–03	Austro-Sardinian War	...	7,000	7,000
1717–17	Spain seizes Sardinia	...	1,000	1,000
1718–20	Spain attacks Austria	...	25,000	25,000
1763–65	France seizes Corsica	...	1,000	1,000
1815–15	Neapolitan War (Aust-Hung)	...	5,000	5,000
1820–21	Lib vs Govt; A-H intervene	2,000	1,000	3,000
1848–48	Lib vs Two Sic; Aust interv.	...	...	1,000
1849–49	France vs Rome; A-H invade	1,000	2,000	3,000
1859–59	A-H vs Italy; Fr intervenes	18,000	22,000	40,000
1860–61	Democ vs Autoc; Fr interv.	0	2,000	2,000
1862–70	Italy vs Papal States	...	8,000	8,000
1915–18	World War I	0	950,000	950,000
1940–45	World War II (Allied 1943–45)	70,000	150,000	220,000
Lithuania				**247,000**
1658–60	Russia vs Poland	...	44,000	44,000
1920–20	Poland vs Lithuania	...	1,000	1,000
1941–41	World War II; Ger kills resisters	200,000	...	200,000
1944–44	World War II; USSR kills collaborators	2,000	...	2,000
Malta				**24,000**
1559–65	Turkey vs Spain	...	24,000	24,000
Netherlands				**1,497,000**
1585–04	Dutch Indep & Span Armada	56,000	121,000	177,000
1652–54	England vs Neth at sea	...	26,000	26,000
1665–67	England vs Netherlands	...	37,000	37,000
1667–68	France vs Spain	...	7,000	7,000
1672–74	UK & France vs Netherlands	...	8,000	8,000
1672–79	France vs Netherlands	...	342,000	342,000
1688–97	France vs Augsberg League	...	680,000	680,000
1780–84	UK vs Netherlands	...	9,000	9,000
1789–90	Dutch Insurrection vs Austria	...	5,000	5,000
1940–45	World War II	200,000	6,000	206,000
Norway				**9,000**
1940–40	World War II	7,000	2,000	9,000
Poland				**7,498,000**
1512–21	Russia vs Poland	...	30,000	30,000
1583–90	Turkey vs Poland	...	17,000	17,000
1632–34	Russia invaded Poland	...	16,000	16,000
1654–56	Russia vs Poland	...	...	8,000
1655–61	Sweden vs Poland	...	30,000	30,000
1715–17	Tarnograd vs Russia	...	6,000	6,000
1733–35	Russia invaded Poland	...	88,000	88,000
1792–94	Polish Revolt & Partition	41,000	4,000	45,000
1794–94	Poland vs Russia & Prussia	...	...	30,000
1831–31	Poles vs Russia	6,000	15,000	21,000
1846–46	Austria vs Poles	1,000	1,000	2,000
1863–64	Poland vs Russia	...	5,000	5,000
1914–18	World War I	500,000	...	500,000
1919–20	USSR vs Poland; Fr interv.	...	100,000	100,000
1939–45	World War II	6,000,000	600,000	6,600,000
Portugal				**117,000**
1579–81	Spain vs Portugal	...	4,000	4,000
1642–68	Port vs Spain for Indep	...	80,000	80,000
1829–34	Conserv vs Gov; UK, Fr, Sp interv.	...	...	20,000
1916–18	World War I	0	13,000	13,000
Romania				**1,297,000**
1784–85	Romanian peasants vs Hung	...	4,000	4,000
1907–07	Peasants vs Govt	...	...	2,000
1916–17	World War I	275,000	375,000	650,000
1941–45	World War II (Allied 1944–45)	300,000	340,000	640,000
1989–89	Govt. vs Demonstrators	1,000	0	1,000
Spain				**1,258,000**
1821–23	Royal vs Govt; Fr invade	5,000	5,000	10,000
1833–40	Carlists vs Govt; UK, Fr, Port interv.	...	...	33,000
1847–49	Carlists vs Government	...	...	3,000
1868–68	Liberals vs Government	...	...	2,000
1872–76	Carlists vs Government	...	...	7,000
1934–34	Asturian miners vs Govt	3,000	...	3,000
1936–39	Civ. War, It, USSR, Ger interv.	600,000	600,000	1,200,000
Sweden				**409,000**
1598–99	Poland invaded Sweden	...	...	1,000
1611–13	Kalmar (Den & Nor v Swed)	...	2,000	2,000
1656–58	Russia vs Sweden	...	8,000	8,000
1700–21	Northern War (Swed vs Russ)	...	382,000	382,000
1741–43	Sweden vs Russia	...	10,000	10,000
1808–09	Russia vs Sweden	...	6,000	6,000
Switzerland				**1,000**
1531–31	Cath. vs Protestant cantons	...	...	1,000
Turkey				**3,297,000**
1559–59	Civil War between brothers	...	...	1,000
1730–30	Janissaries Revolt	...	7,000	7,000
1806–12	Russia vs Turkey	...	45,000	45,000
1826–26	Janissaries massacred	14,000	6,000	20,000
1828–29	Russia vs Turkey	61,000	130,000	191,000
1877–78	Russia vs Turkey	...	285,000	285,000
1889–89	Cretan revolt vs Turkey	2,000	1,000	3,000
1894–97	Armenians vs Turkey	39,000	1,000	40,000
1897–97	Greece vs Turk over Crete	...	...	2,000
1909–10	Massacres in Armenia	6,000	0	6,000
1911–12	Italy vs Turkey	...	20,000	20,000
1912–13	1st Balkan War vs Turkey	...	82,000	82,000
1914–18	World War I	1,000,000	450,000	1,450,000
1915–16	Armenians deported	1,000,000	...	1,000,000
1919–20	France vs Turkey	...	...	40,000
1919–22	Greece vs Turkey	50,000	50,000	100,000
1977–80	Terrorism; mil coup 1980	...	...	5,000
United Kingdom				**1,612,000**
1513–15	Scotland vs England	...	10,000	10,000
1522–23	England vs Scotland	...	3,000	3,000
1542–50	England vs Scotland	...	13,000	13,000
1547–50	Arundel's Rebellion	...	6,000	6,000
1554–54	Wyatt's Rebellion	...	1,000	1,000
1560–60	Scots & UK vs France	...	6,000	6,000
1667–68	Scottish Rebellion vs UK	...	...	2,000
1642–46	Parliament vs King	25,000	25,000	50,000
1649–50	Irish Rebellion vs UK	2,000	1,000	3,000
1650–51	UK vs Scotland	...	8,000	8,000
1679–79	Covenanter rebel vs UK	...	2,000	2,000
1689–91	Irish vs English (Fr interv.)	...	7,000	7,000
1715–15	Scotland vs UK	...	...	2,000
1726–29	Spanish-British War	...	15,000	15,000
1745–46	Scots try to seize power	...	3,000	3,000
1914–18	World War I	31,000	1,000,000	1,031,000
1939–45	World War II	100,000	350,000	450,000
USSR				**24,928,000**
1570–70	Russia sacks Novgorod	60,000	...	60,000
1571–72	Tartars vs Moscow	...	...	1,000
1608–12	Poland invaded Russia	...	37,000	37,000
1614–21	Poland vs Turkey in Ukraine	...	15,000	15,000
1671–76	Turkey vs Poland in Ukraine	...	25,000	25,000
1678–81	Turkey vs Russia in Ukraine	...	12,000	12,000
1695–96	Russia vs Turkey at Azov	...	30,000	30,000
1698–98	Streltsy Revolt vs Czar	...	1,000	1,000
1716–17	Russian expedition to Khiva	...	2,000	2,000
1773–74	Cossack & Peasant Revolt	16,000	2,000	18,000
1829–40	Circassians vs USSR	9,000	1,000	10,000
1839–39	Russia vs Khivans	1,000	4,000	5,000
1853–56	Turk v Rus; UK, Fr, It invad.	508,000	264,000	772,000
1865–76	Russia expanded to Cen Asia	...	11,000	11,000
1878–81	Russia vs Turkomans	20,000	1,000	21,000
1904–05	Japan vs Russia	...	130,000	130,000
1905–05	Pogrom, Russians vs Jews	2,000	0	2,000
1905–06	Peasants & Workers vs Govt	1,000	0	1,000
1914–17	World War I	3,000,000	2,950,000	5,950,000
1916–16	Kirghiz massacre Russians	...	...	9,000
1917–17	Bourgeois rev vs Czar	1,000	1,000	2,000
1918–20	Civ War; US, UK, Fr, Jap interv.	500,000	300,000	800,000
1939–39	Japan vs USSR	0	13,000	13,000
1941–45	World War II	8,500,000	8,500,000	17,000,000
1969–69	China attack USSR border	...	1,000	1,000
Yugoslavia				**2,259,000**
1836–37	Bosnia vs Turkey	...	...	2,000
1841–41	Bosnia vs Turkey	1,000	0	1,000
1852–53	Turkey vs Montenegro	3,000	5,000	8,000
1858–59	Turkey vs Montenegro	...	3,000	3,000
1862–62	Christians vs Turkey	2,000	0	2,000
1903–03	Macedonian revolt vs Turk	2,000	2,000	4,000
1913–13	2nd Balkan War vs Bulgar	...	61,000	61,000
1914–18	World War I	650,000	128,000	778,000
1941–45	World War II	1,000,000	400,000	1,400,000
Europe (area-wide)				**21,569,000**
1701–14	Spain vs Grand Alliance	...	1,251,000	1,251,000
1755–63	7-Year War (Eur, N Am, India)	370,000	988,000	1,358,000
1803–15	Napoleonic Wars	1,000,000	1,869,000	2,869,000
1914–18	World War I area-wide[3]	5,982,000	401,000	6,383,000
1939–45	World War II Eur area-wide[3]	8,723,000	985,000	9,708,000
Middle East		464,000	709,000	1,235,000
Cyprus				**60,000**
1570–78	Turkey vs Spain & Italy	...	55,000	55,000
1974–74	Natl Guard; Turk invasion	3,000	2,000	5,000
Egypt				**84,000**
1807–07	UK Expedition to Egypt	...	1,000	1,000
1820–21	Egypt conquered Nubians	1,000	1,000	2,000
1878–79	Egypt vs slave-raiders	...	...	1,000
1882–82	Egypt vs UK	1,000	0	1,000
1956–56	Suez; Is, Fr, UK invasion	1,000	3,000	4,000
1967–67	Six-Day War; border conflicts	50,000	25,000	75,000
Iran				**672,000**
1510–10	Iran vs Uzbeks	...	...	1,000
1514–17	Turkey vs Iran & Egypt	...	...	39,000
1722–23	Russo–Iran War	...	4,000	4,000
1795–96	Russo–Iran War	...	2,000	2,000
1804–13	Russo–Iran War	...	26,000	26,000

Wars and War-Related Deaths, 1500–1990

Location and Identification of Conflict[1]	Number of Deaths Civilian	Military	Total
1821–22 Turkey vs Iran	1,000	0	1,000
1826–28 Russia vs Iran	2,000	5,000	7,000
1856–57 UK vs Iran	1,000	2,000	3,000
1908–09 Constitutionalists vs Govt; USSR interv.	...		1,000
1978–89 Islam vs Shah; dissidents	70,000	18,000	88,000
1980–88 Iraq vs Iran	50,000	450,000	500,000
Iraq			**120,000**
1920–21 Arabs vs UK	1,000	1,000	2,000
1933–33 Kurd massacred Christians	1,000	0	1,000
1959–59 Shammar Tribe vs Govt	1,000	1,000	2,000
1961–70 Kurds vs Govt; Iran interv.	100,000	5,000	105,000
1988–88 Kurd civs killed by army	9,000	1,000	10,000
Israel			**24,000**
1948–48 Arab League vs Israel	0	8,000	8,000
1973–73 Yom Kippur War vs Egypt, Syria	0	16,000	16,000
Jordan			**10,000**
1970–70 Palestinians & Syr vs Govt	5,000	5,000	10,000
Kuwait			**1,000**
1990–90 Iraq invaded Kuwait	1,000	0	1,000
Lebanon			**168,000**
1860–60 Muslims massacred Christians	3,000	0	3,000
1958–58 US intervene in civil war	1,000	1,000	2,000
1975–76 Syria intervene in civ war	75,000	25,000	100,000
1982–90 Israel invaded Lebanon & aftermath	41,000	22,000	63,000
Palestine			**1,000**
1834–34 Palestine vs Egypt	1,000	0	1,000
Syria			**66,000**
1820–20 Turkey vs Arabs	1,000	0	1,000
1831–32 Eg vs Turk; Rus, Fr, UK interv.	8,000	10,000	18,000
1839–40 Eg vs Turk & UK; Ger, Rus, Fr interv.	2,000	10,000	12,000
1845–45 Maronite vs Druse; Turk interv.	1,000	0	1,000
1896–96 Druses vs Turkey	1,000	0	1,000
1920–20 France vs Syria	...	...	5,000
1925–27 Druses vs France	4,000	4,000	8,000
1982–82 Govt massacre Conserv Muslims	20,000	0	20,000
Yemen			**30,000**
1948–48 Yahya family vs N. Yemen	2,000	2,000	4,000
1962–69 Civ war in N. Yem.; Egypt interv.	...	...	15,000
1986–87 Civil War in South Yemen	7,000	4,000	11,000
South Asia	**2,302,000**	**1,171,000**	**3,610,000**
Afghanistan			**1,337,000**
1837–38 Iran vs Afghanistan	...	...	1,000
1838–42 UK vs Afghanistan	10,000	10,000	20,000
1878–80 UK vs Afghanistan	...	4,000	4,000
1885–85 Russia vs Afghanistan	...	1,000	1,000
1919–19 Afghanistan vs UK	0	1,000	1,000
1924–25 Anti–Reform vs Govt; UK interv.	1,000	1,000	2,000
1928–29 Anti–Reform vs Govt	4,000	4,000	8,000
1978–89 USSR intervened in civ war	800,000	500,000	1,300,000
Bangladesh			**1,000,000**
1971–71 India intervene; fam & mas	500,000	500,000	1,000,000
Bhutan			**1,000**
1864–65 UK vs Bhutan	...	...	1,000
India			**1,223,000**
1508–09 Gujerat–Egypt vs Portugal	...	...	2,000
1509–12 Portuguese conquered Goa	...	...	3,000
1525–26 Mogul vs Delhi	...	15,000	15,000
1526–29 Rajput vs Mogul	...	...	45,000
1537–39 Afghans vs Moguls	...	...	2,000
1565–65 Muslims vs Vijayanagar	...	...	1,000
1622–23 Iran vs Mogul Empire	...	...	1,000
1657–59 Civil War of 4 brothers	...	...	2,000
1708–08 Mogul Civil War	...	...	1,000
1738–39 Iran invaded Mogul India	20,000	...	20,000
1756–57 Bengal vs UK	...	...	1,000
1758–61 Afghanistan capture Delhi	...	...	75,000
1763–65 Bengal Rulers vs UK	...	3,000	3,000
1778–81 UK vs Marathas	...	3,000	3,000
1782–84 UK East India Co vs Mysore	...	2,000	2,000
1790–92 UK East India Co vs Mysore	...	2,000	2,000
1792–99 Tippu Sahib vs UK	...	7,000	7,000
1802–06 Marathas vs UK	...	4,000	4,000
1802–02 Maratha Civil War	...	...	1,000
1806–06 Sepoy Revolt vs UK	...	1,000	1,000
1814–17 Gurkhas vs UK	...	3,000	3,000
1817–18 UK conquered Marathas	2,000	2,000	4,000
1825–26 UK besieged Bharatpur	4,000	1,000	5,000
1843–43 UK vs Baluchis, Sind Army	5,000	1,000	6,000
1845–46 UK vs Sikhs	3,000	5,000	8,000
1848–49 Sikhs vs UK	8,000	2,000	10,000
1852–52 Dards vs Dogras	2,000	0	2,000
1855–55 Santals vs UK	1,000	0	1,000
1857–59 Sepoy mutiny vs UK	11,000	4,000	15,000
1863–63 Muslim rebellion vs UK	1,000	0	1,000
1897–98 Muslim rebellion vs UK	...	...	1,000
1914–18 World War I	25,000	25,000	50,000
1918–19 Amritsar massacre by UK	1,000	0	1,000
1921–22 UK intervene in civil war	11,000	0	11,000
1936–38 UK intervene in civil war	11,000	0	11,000
1939–45 World War II	25,000	24,000	49,000
1946–48 Muslim vs Hindu; UK inter	800,000	0	800,000
1947–49 Muslims, Pak vs Kashmir (India)	1,000	2,000	3,000
1948–48 India vs Hyderabad	1,000	1,000	2,000
1962–62 China vs India at border	1,000	1,000	2,000
1965–65 Pak vs Kashmir (India interv.)	13,000	7,000	20,000
1971–71 Pakistan vs India; border war	...	11,000	11,000
1983–90 Ethnic & political violence	12,000	4,000	16,000
Pakistan			**9,000**
1973–77 Baluchis v Govt; Afgh interv.	6,000	3,000	9,000
Sri Lanka			**40,000**
1971–71 Maoists vs Govt	5,000	5,000	10,000
1984–90 Tamils vs Sinhalese vs Govt	18,000	12,000	30,000

Location and Identification of Conflict[1]	Number of Deaths Civilian	Military	Total
Far East	**16,513,000**	**13,398,000**	**31,185,000**
Burma			**49,000**
1823–26 UK conquered Burma	5,000	15,000	20,000
1852–53 Burma vs UK	...	...	1,000
1885–86 UK annexed Burma	...	...	6,000
1948–51 Karens vs Govt; China interv.	...	...	8,000
1980–80 Communists vs Govt	...	...	5,000
1985–88 Rebels vs Govt	6,000	3,000	9,000
Cambodia			**1,221,000**
1970–75 NV & US intervene civil war	78,000	78,000	156,000
1975–78 Pol Pot famine & massacre	750,000	250,000	1,000,000
1978–89 Vietnam vs Cambodia	14,000	51,000	65,000
China			**18,749,000**
1716–18 Dzungars invaded Tibet	...	1,000	1,000
1755–57 China vs Dzungars; massacres	300,000	300,000	600,000
1765–70 Burma invade China border	...	40,000	40,000
1771–76 Revolt in Szechwan	60,000	60,000	120,000
1774–74 Revolt of Shantung	15,000	15,000	30,000
1795–97 Miao–tseu Rebellion	10,000	5,000	15,000
1807–07 Koukou–Nor natives rebel	...	...	5,000
1822–28 Kashgaria Revolt	...	...	25,000
1826–28 Muslim uprising	...	...	20,000
1830–30 Kokanese invasion	...	...	1,000
1839–42 UK vs China (Opium War)	1,000	10,000	11,000
1841–41 Dogras vs Tibet	3,000	1,000	4,000
1847–48 China vs Kashgaria	...	...	1,000
1856–60 UK & Fr vs China (Opium)	10,000	1,000	11,000
1857–57 China vs Kashgaria	...	...	2,000
1860–72 Muslim rebellions vs China	...	...	300,000
1860–64 Taiping rebel; UK, Fr interv.	5,000,000	5,000,000	10,000,000
1884–85 France vs China	...	...	12,000
1894–95 Japan vs China over Korea	...	15,000	15,000
1900–00 Manchuria vs Russ occupation	...	...	4,000
1900–00 Boxer rebel (5 nations invade)	13,000	3,000	16,000
1904–04 UK expedition to Tibet	...	...	1,000
1911–11 Republicans vs Govt	1,000	1,000	2,000
1912–13 Tibet vs China	...	...	2,000
1913–13 Republicans vs Govt	5,000	5,000	10,000
1913–14 Bandits vs Govt	5,000	5,000	10,000
1914–14 Pai–Lings vs Govt	...	...	5,000
1917–18 Yunnan revolt	...	...	1,000
1917–18 Szechuanese vs others	1,000	1,000	2,000
1918–18 Tibet vs China; UK interv	0	1,000	1,000
1920–20 Szechuanese vs others	2,000	2,000	4,000
1926–28 Civ War; USSR, Jap interv.	...	...	10,000
1928–28 Muslim rebellion vs Govt	...	...	200,000
1929–30 Warlords vs Govt	...	...	75,000
1929–29 USSR vs China	0	3,000	3,000
1930–35 Communists vs Govt	...	...	500,000
1931–34 USSR intervene Turkistan	...	...	20,000
1931–33 Japan vs Manchuria	...	60,000	60,000
1937–41 Japan vs China	1,150,000	650,000	1,800,000
1941–45 World War II	850,000	1,350,000	2,200,000
1946–50 Comm vs Kuomint; US interv	500,000	500,000	1,000,000
1950–51 Govt executes landlords	1,000,000	...	1,000,000
1950–51 China vs Tibet	2,000	0	2,000
1956–59 Tibetan Revolt	60,000	40,000	100,000
1967–68 Cultural Revolution	450,000	50,000	500,000
1983–84 Govt executions	5,000	0	5,000
1989–89 Government killed students	1,000	0	1,000
1990–90 Government executions	2,000	0	2,000
Indonesia			**910,000**
1825–25 Bonian rev vs Netherlands	1,000	0	1,000
1825–30 Java revolt vs Netherlands	...	15,000	15,000
1845–45 UK vs Borneo Pirates	...	...	1,000
1859–60 Bonian rev vs Netherlands	1,000	0	1,000
1873–78 Achinese vs Netherlands	150,000	50,000	200,000
1894–94 Netherlands vs Bali	...	...	1,000
1945–46 Independence from Neth, UK	4,000	1,000	5,000
1950–50 Moluccans vs Govt	...	...	5,000
1953–53 Darul Islam vs Govt	...	...	1,000
1958–60 Dissident Military vs Govt	...	...	30,000
1965–66 Abortive coup; US interv.	500,000	...	500,000
1975–82 Annex E. Timor; fam & mass	100,000	50,000	150,000
Japan			**2,027,000**
1863–63 UK, Fr, US exped to Japan	1,000	...	1,000
1877–77 Satsuma rebellion	...	...	14,000
1923–23 Massacre of Koreans	10,000	0	10,000
1938–38 USSR vs Japan	...	2,000	2,000
1941–45 World War II	500,000	1,500,000	2,000,000
Korea			**3,002,000**
1948–48 Army vs Govt	0	1,000	1,000
1950–53 Korean War; Ch, US interv.	1,500,000	1,500,000	3,000,000
1980–80 SK Army killed people	1,000	0	1,000
Laos			**30,000**
1960–73 Pathet Lao vs Gov; US bomb, NV invad.	18,000	12,000	30,000
Malaysia			**13,000**
1950–60 UK intervened in civil war	...	...	13,000
Mongolia			**31,000**
1939–39 Japan vs Mongolia & USSR	...	28,000	28,000
1945–45 World War II	0	3,000	3,000
Philippines			**408,000**
1896–98 Phil vs Spain; US invaded	...	2,000	2,000
1899–02 Philippine revolt vs US	200,000	4,000	204,000
1941–45 World War II	91,000	27,000	118,000
1950–52 Huks vs Govt	5,000	4,000	9,000
1972–89 Muslims vs Govt; US interv.	20,000	15,000	35,000
1972–89 Comm vs Govt; US interv.	20,000	20,000	40,000
Taiwan			**26,000**
1947–47 Taiwan vs China	0	1,000	1,000
1947–47 Civilian riots vs govt	20,000	0	20,000
1954–55 Civil strife	...	...	5,000
Thailand			**5,000**
1893–93 France vs Siam	...	1,000	1,000
1940–41 France vs Thailand	2,000	2,000	4,000

Wars and War-Related Deaths, 1500–1990

Location and Identification of Conflict[1]		Number of Deaths Civilian	Military	Total
Vietnam				**3,084,000**
1788–89	Chinese exped to Annam	...	30,000	30,000
1795–03	White Lotus Uprising	10,000	10,000	20,000
1858–62	France invade Cochinchina		4,000	4,000
1873–85	France conquered Tonkin	15,000	15,000	30,000
1882–85	France vs Annam; China interv.	2,000	4,000	6,000
1945–54	Indep. vs Fr; Ch, US interv.	300,000	300,000	600,000
1960–65	US intervene in civil war	200,000	100,000	300,000
1965–75	US & SV vs NV	1,000,000	1,058,000	2,058,000
1979–79	China vs Vietnam	9,000	26,000	35,000
1987–87	China vs Vietnam–border	0	1,000	1,000
Asia (area-wide)				**1,630,000**
1941–45	World War II in Asia	1,534,000	96,000	1,630,000
Oceania		**50,000**	**137,000**	**187,000**
Australia				**94,000**
1914–18	World War I	0	60,000	60,000
1939–45	World War II	0	34,000	34,000
New Zealand				**93,000**
1860–70	2nd Maori War vs UK	50,000	10,000	60,000
1914–18	World War I	0	16,000	16,000
1939–45	World War II	0	17,000	17,000
Sub–Saharan Africa		**4,806,000**	**1,597,000**	**6,625,000**
Angola				**396,000**
1961–75	Inde vs Port; USSR, S Af interv.	30,000	25,000	55,000
1975–90	Cuba & S Af intervened civ war	320,000	21,000	341,000
Benin				**3,000**
1889–92	Dahomey revolt vs France		3,000	3,000
Burundi				**115,000**
1972–72	Hutus vs Govt; massacres	100,000	10,000	110,000
1988–88	Tutsi massacred Hutu civs	5,000	0	5,000
Cameroon				**32,000**
1955–60	Independence vs France, UK	...	...	32,000
Chad				**11,000**
1893–93	Rabeh vs Bornu	...	...	4,000
1980–87	Reb vs Govt; Fr, Libya interv.	2,000	5,000	7,000
Ethiopia				**674,000**
1861–61	King killed rebels; Fr interv.	...	...	2,000
1867–68	UK invaded to free captives	4,000	0	4,000
1867–67	Civil War			3,000
1875–76	Egypt vs Ethiopia			7,000
1895–96	Italy vs Ethiopia	10,000	9,000	19,000
1935–36	Italy vs Ethiopia	...	20,000	20,000
1941–41	World War II	5,000	5,000	10,000
1974–90	Eritrean revolt & famine	500,000	70,000	570,000
1976–83	Cuba & Somalia intervened	15,000	24,000	39,000
Ghana				**6,000**
1824–25	UK conquered Ashantis	3,000	0	3,000
1873–74	Ashantis vs UK	1,000	0	1,000
1893–94	3rd Ashanti War vs UK	...	1,000	1,000
1981–81	Konkomba vs Nanumba	...	...	1,000
Guinea–Bissau				**15,000**
1962–74	Independence vs Portugal	5,000	10,000	15,000
Ivory Coast				**1,000**
1885–86	France defeated Ivory tribe	...	1,000	1,000
Kenya				**16,000**
1895–96	UK vs Kenya	1,000	0	1,000
1952–63	Independence from UK	3,000	12,000	15,000
Liberia				**11,000**
1985–85	Reprisal for Coup Attempt	5,000		5,000
1990–90	Rebels vs Rebels vs Govt	9,000	1,000	10,000
Madagascar				**25,000**
1883–85	Madagascar revolt France	...	2,000	2,000
1894–95	France annexed Madagascar	2,000	6,000	8,000
1947–48	Independence from France	10,000	5,000	15,000
Mozambique				**1,080,000**
1965–75	Independence vs Portugal	...	...	30,000
1981–90	Famine worsened by civ war	1,000,000	50,000	1,050,000
Namibia				**80,000**
1903–08	SW Af rev vs Germ; massacres	80,000	...	80,000
Nigeria				**2,007,000**
1897–97	UK vs Nigeria; Fr interv.	1,000	0	1,000
1967–70	Biafrans vs Govt; fam & mass	1,000,000	1,000,000	2,000,000
1980–81	Fundamental Islam vs Govt	...	...	5,000
1984–84	Fundamental Islam vs Govt	...	...	1,000
Rwanda				**105,000**
1956–65	Tutsis vs Govt; massacres	102,000	3,000	105,000
Senegal				**2,000**
1857–57	France vs Senegal	1,000	0	1,000
1890–91	France vs Senegal	...		1,000
Sierra Leone				**2,000**
1898–98	Sierra Leone Tribes vs UK	2,000	0	2,000
Somalia				**55,000**
1988–90	Civil War in north	50,000	5,000	55,000
Sudan				**1,062,000**
1869–69	Blacks vs Arabs	...	...	1,000
1882–85	Mahdist rebel UK; Eg interv.	8,000	20,000	28,000
1884–85	Sudan massacred garrison	...	1,000	1,000
1885–95	Sudan vs Egypt and UK	9,000	1,000	10,000
1896–99	Egypt and UK vs Sudan	15,000	1,000	16,000
1963–72	Black vs Govt; UK, Eg interv.	250,000	250,000	500,000
1984–90	Blacks vs Islamic Law	500,000	6,000	506,000
Tanzania				**155,000**
1888–93	Arab & Black vs Germany	...	5,000	5,000
1905–07	Revolt vs Germ; massacres	150,000	0	150,000

Location and Identification of Conflict[1]		Number of Deaths Civilian	Military	Total
Uganda				**615,000**
1880–80	Ceremonial massacre	...	...	1,000
1893–93	Army vs King	...	...	1,000
1966–66	Buganda Tribe vs Govt	1,000	1,000	2,000
1971–78	Idi Amin massacres	300,000	0	300,000
1978–79	Tanz vs Amin; Libya interv.	...	3,000	3,000
1981–87	Army vs people; massacres	300,000	8,000	308,000
West Sahara				**16,000**
1975–87	Independence from Morocco	3,000	13,000	16,000
Zaire				**120,000**
1892–94	Belgium vs Arabs	...	...	20,000
1960–65	UK, Bel intervene, Katanga	...	...	100,000
Zambia				**1,000**
1964–64	Civil strife			1,000
Zimbabwe				**16,000**
1972–79	Patriot Front vs Rhodesia	...	...	12,000
1983–83	Political violence	2,000	0	2,000
1983–84	Ethnic violence; Af. interv.	2,000	0	2,000
Other Africa[4]		**442,000**	**202,000**	**837,000**
Algeria				**416,000**
1541–41	Spain vs Algeria	0	7,000	7,000
1775–75	Spain invade Algeria	...	3,000	3,000
1839–47	France vs Algeria	285,000	15,000	300,000
1856–57	Kabylia uprising vs Fran	...	...	1,000
1871–72	Algeria vs France	...	...	1,000
1945–45	France intervene in civil	2,000	0	2,000
1954–62	France intervene in civil	82,000	18,000	100,000
1962–63	Rebel leaders vs Govt	1,000	1,000	2,000
Libya				**96,000**
1911–17	UK, Italy intervene in civ	...	...	16,000
1920–32	Italian conquest of Libya	...	...	40,000
1930–32	Italy intervene in civil war	...	...	40,000
Morocco				**79,000**
1578–78	Portugal vs Morocco	...	8,000	8,000
1775–75	Spanish–Moroccan War	...	1,000	1,000
1859–60	Sp vs Mor; Fr, UK intervene	...	10,000	10,000
1907–08	France intervene in civil	1,000	...	1,000
1909–10	France intervene in civil	1,000	1,000	2,000
1909–10	Spain vs Morocco	0	10,000	10,000
1911–11	France intervene in civil	1,000	1,000	2,000
1916–17	France intervene in civil	1,000	1,000	2,000
1921–26	France & Spain intervene	11,000	29,000	40,000
1953–56	Indep from Fr; Spain interv.	3,000	0	3,000
South Africa				**213,000**
1818–28	Shaka Zulu Expansion	...	...	85,000
1836–37	Boers vs Matabele	...	...	1,000
1837–37	Matabele vs Ma–Kalanga	...	...	1,000
1838–40	Whites & Blacks vs Zulus	15,000	1,000	16,000
1840–40	Matabele vs Mashonas	...	...	1,000
1846–47	South Af. Kaffirs vs UK	...	1,000	1,000
1850–53	8th South Af Kaffir War	...	3,000	3,000
1854–54	Bantu vs Boers	3,000	0	3,000
1856–56	Zulu Civil War (brothers)	...	...	1,000
1877–78	9th Kaffir War vs UK	...	1,000	1,000
1879–79	UK vs Zulus	1,000	3,000	4,000
1880–81	Basuto revolt vs UK	...	1,000	1,000
1880–81	Transvaal revolt vs UK	...	18,000	18,000
1899–02	Boer independence vs UK	20,000	32,000	52,000
1906–06	Zulu revolt vs UK	...	...	5,000
1939–45	World War II	0	9,000	9,000
1976–76	Blacks vs Security Forces	1,000	0	1,000
1983–90	Black vs Black vs Police	10,000	0	10,000
Tunisia				**33,000**
1532–35	Spain vs Turkey	...	28,000	28,000
1535–35	Spain vs Tunisia	...	...	1,000
1881–81	France vs Tunisia	1,000	0	1,000
1952–54	Independence from France	3,000	0	3,000
TOTAL DEATHS, 1500–1990		**75,649,000[5]**	**63,709,000[5]**	**141,901,000**

... Not available

1. Location refers to country which was principal battleground, except for two World Wars for which location refers to participating country.

2. Argentina, Bolivia, Chile, Colombia (including present Panama and Venezuela), Paraguay, Peru, Uruguay.

3. World War area-wide deaths are in addition to those which could be located by country, and are shown under the country of origin.

4. Egypt is shown under Middle East.

5. Incomplete; breakdown of civilian and military deaths not available in all cases.

> **War**—any armed conflict involving one or more governments and causing the death of 1,000 or more people per year.
>
> **Intervention**—overt military action by foreign forces, at the invitation of the government in power.
>
> **Invasion**—armed attack by foreign country, including air attack without land invasion.

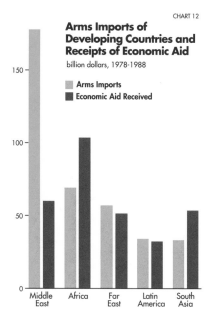

CHART 12

Arms Imports of Developing Countries and Receipts of Economic Aid

billion dollars, 1978-1988

■ Arms Imports
■ Economic Aid Received

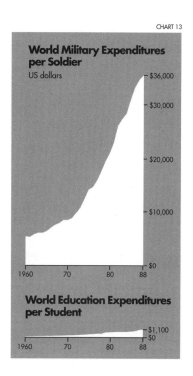

CHART 13

World Military Expenditures per Soldier

US dollars

World Education Expenditures per Student

Military and Social Connections

The aftermath of a war can be revealing, pointing up major problems that the war has left unresolved or that the war itself has created. For a war may be a military success but a social disaster, leaving in its wake a fitful peace: infrastructure and sources of food and water destroyed, starvation and epidemics rampant, thousands of innocent bystanders killed or wounded. (The 16 wars that were going on in 1990 had already killed 2,632,000 civilians.) War makes the conflict between military objectives and social needs glaringly obvious. The impact on society's well-being is visual and unmistakable.

It is much more difficult to see the military-social connections during the peacetime preparations for war. The ordinary humdrum activities associated with the world's annual expenditures on military "defense"—i.e., training armies, piloting jets, producing weapons, exporting arms—are less obvious in their impact on social development. They produce no clear visual connections, no evident death and destruction. Yet these activities have a singularly negative effect on society's ability to make tangible and equitable progress.

Military depredations against the environment, the economy, and political freedoms occur in peace as well as in war. Activities related to military defense have direct effects on personal health through the build-up of nuclear and other toxic wastes, training flights, deforestation, the movement of hazardous substances. Those activities also weaken democracy through the emphasis they give to central political control and the hallowed secrecy that marks military plans and operations.

The impact on the economy is also negative and has tended to become a heavier burden over time. In recent decades military expenditures have taken $5 of every $100 of goods and services produced in the world, a share of gross product five times as large as that allocated to defense before World War II. In terms of revenues and expenditures the military drain is enormous: $15 to $20 of every $100 spent by central governments now goes to military purposes, triple their budgets for education, eight times their budgets for housing.

Comparative public budgets are, in fact, good clues not only to the broad military-social connections but also to the specifics of government policies. Close scrutiny often reveals a world of grossly distorted priorities. The two charts on this page are illustrative.

Aid and arms trade—Despite the desperate need for development progress in the Third World, developing countries as a group spent 23 percent more of their resources to procure foreign weapons from 1978 to 1988 than they received in economic development aid (*chart 12*). That almost half of those arms purchases were made by the Middle East seems less surprising than that the ratio between arms bought and foreign aid received was as close as it appears to have been in the other Third World regions, which had lower income per capita. In effect the arms purchases overall cancelled out the stimulus to development intended in the aid program.

This would be even more shocking if it were not for the fact that the aid flow from the developed countries was no torrent. Their total investment in the development of the power countries in this period actually was very little more than the income they had from the sale of arms to those countries.

Students and soldiers—The rise in world population continues to exceed the public funds available to provide primary education for all. Since 1960 the world's school-age population has increased by 600 million, the number enrolled in school by 450 million. The number of adult illiterates has also grown and now stands at 900 million. The most severe educational shortages are, of course, in the developing world, where large numbers of children lack access to even minimal school facilities. But in many developed countries, too, higher priorities for education are urgently needed to provide quality improvements, ranging from functional literacy to math and science skills.

It is against this background that the disparity between public funds expended per soldier and per student must be seen (*chart 13*). Public expenditures for education have increased sharply since 1960; in fact, they have grown more than military expenditures and now exceed them (*chart 1*, page 6). But the budget to meet education needs is a moving target; today there are 68 percent more children of school age than there were 30 years ago.

For military objectives, governments now invest an average of $36,000 per year per member of the armed forces, thirty times more than they invest in the education of a child enrolled in school. The formidable gap between the two underscores the serious neglect of human capital, and with it, of economic development, in favor of unlimited military power.

Military expenditures and productivity—The neglect of human capital translates into the neglect of economic development, because it is on the human factor that society's growth ultimately depends. *Chart 14* shows a pattern which *WMSE* has illustrated several times in the past. Major industrial countries with high rates of military expenditures are associated with low growth in productivity. For the superpowers the negative correlation is striking: the US, which has spent an average of 6.4 percent of GNP on the military since 1960, shows an annual rate of productivity growth of only 2.8 percent; the USSR, with an average 10.5 percent devoted to the military, has—according to CIA estimates—the lowest productivity growth of all, just 2.4 percent.

At the opposite end of the scale is Japan. Still subsidized by US military protection and carrying a low military burden of 0.9 percent of its GNP, Japan has enjoyed an annual average 7.8 percent rise in productivity—and with it fast economic growth and a highly favorable competitive position in international markets.

CHART 14

Military Expenditures and Productivity 1960-1988

Military Expenditures
percent of GNP

Manufacturing Productivity
annual rate of growth

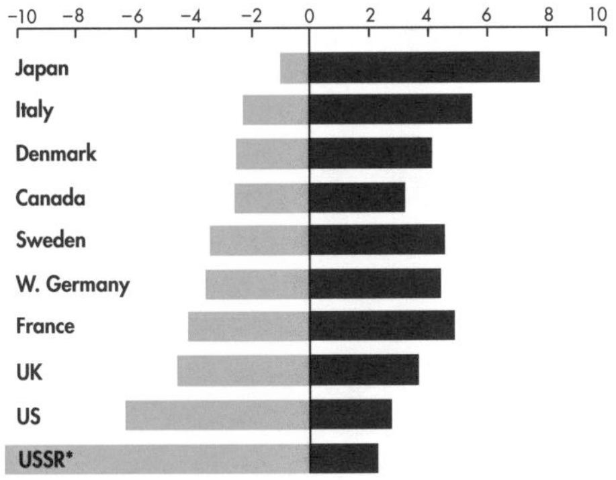

*1962-1988

TWELVE MAJOR MILITARY POWERS

And Their Rank in Social Development and the Environment, 1987

	Military Expenditures	Economic-Social Standing[1]	GNP Per Capita	Education	Health	Environment[2]
	Million US $	RANK AMONG 142 COUNTRIES				
United States	293,211	1	9	8	8	16	135
USSR	274,740	2	19	26	15	30	136
France	34,859	3	10	12	15	11	129
W. Germany	34,135	4	11	9	21	9	125
United Kingdom	31,489	5	16	21	16	22	131
Japan	24,198	6	7	5	14	12	127
Iran	19,000	7	72	60	72	76	95
Italy	18,354	8	25	19	40	23	114
Saudia Arabia	16,500	9	52	33	69	57	137
China	13,418	10	91	117	73	72	122
India	9,815	11	110	114	102	96	115
Iraq	9,370	12	72	59	74	76	108

[1]Summarizes a country's rank among 142 countries in economic-social development. Three factors are combined: GNP per capita, and averages for health and education based on four indicators for each.

[2]Summarizes a country's rank among the 137 countries for which at least four environmental indicators are available. Since statistical coverage of environmental hazards on a global basis is still limited, this selection tends to emphasize population growth and energy intensity.

See pages 54–59 and statistical note, page 61.

The military-social gap—In summary, when military spending is high, economic and social well-being lags. This is also the message conveyed by comparisons of the rankings of 142 countries.

Of the twelve countries with the largest military expenditures in 1987, all made a poorer showing in economic-social standing than in military power. For the developing countries among them, the gap was especially large.

All twelve also made a particularly poor showing in ratings of environmental impact, e.g.: deforestation, energy use, greenhouse gas emissions. Of the 137 countries for which environmental indicators are available, Saudi Arabia ranked the lowest; next in bottom rank were USSR and US.

Compared with 1975, the first year for which *WMSE* provided a development index by country, seven of these twelve countries have dropped in economic-social rank; three are unchanged; only two, Japan and Saudi Arabia, have advanced in comparative economic-social standing.

The Health of the Planet

More than two thousand years ago, King Pyrrhus of Epirus surveyed the carnage on the battlefield at Asculum where his troops had prevailed and uttered, "Another such victory . . . and we are undone." Examining the economic boom and ecological bust that have marked our century, similar thoughts are unavoidable.

The world is rich beyond the wildest dreams of its ancestors. The average person living today spends as much money in a decade as his great-grandparents did in their entire lifetimes. Since 1900, the annual value of goods and services produced worldwide has grown twentyfold (after allowance for inflation), the use of energy thirtyfold, the products of industry fiftyfold, and the average distance traveled by the well-to-do perhaps a thousandfold.

Yet our economic success is wreaking havoc on the earth. Never before has human activity threatened the habitability of so much of the planet. The earth's forests are shrinking, its deserts expanding, and its soils eroding—all at record rates. Each year thousands of plant and animal species disappear, many before they are named or catalogued. The ozone layer in the upper atmosphere that protects us from ultraviolet radiation is thinning.

As human economies pump billions of tons of heat-trapping carbon dioxide into the atmosphere, the very temperature of the earth appears to be rising, posing a threat of unknown dimensions to virtually all the life-support systems on which humanity depends. Carbon dioxide emissions from fossil fuels, the prime culprit among the so-called greenhouse gases, have gone from near zero a century ago to more than a ton of carbon per person on the planet today. The share of emissions from oil—the most versatile of fossil fuels, and the fuel most plagued by political volatility since the 1970s—has grown particularly rapidly in the past half century (*chart 15*).

The planet's natural systems suffer these maladies in direct proportion not only to our growing riches but also to our growing numbers; we have more than doubled our population from 2.5 billion at mid-century to 5.3 billion today. The growth of the world's forces of war over the same period has also exacerbated environmental decline, directly, for example, through scorched-earth warfare and indirectly through the diversion of talent and money away from environmental and other needs.

The remedies required to keep the earth's health from deteriorating into a crisis condition are challenging but not mysterious. They include slowing population growth, reforesting the earth, weaning societies from their reliance on fossil fuels, and reducing global inequity through debt reduction, since the growing gap between rich and poor is a major cause of ecological decline.

If we fail to treat the ailments that imperil the biosphere, ecological decline will inevitably lead to economic decline, and eventually to political and social disintegration. The bulk of scientific findings and recent events suggest that the time remaining to reverse the trends is more accurately measured in years than in decades. If the 1990s are not the turnaround decade they may seal our fate.

Prepared by **Alan B. Durning,** senior researcher at Worldwatch Institute in Washington, D.C. Mr. Durning drew on the work of many of his colleagues at the Institute for this summary; he is coauthor of four of the Institute's annual *State of the World* reports, and author most recently of Worldwatch Paper 95, *Apartheid's Environmental Toll.*

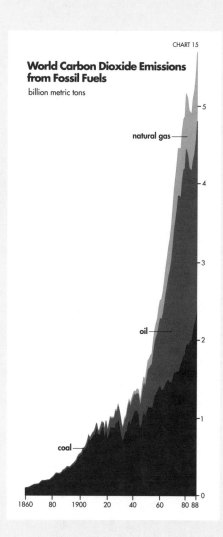

CHART 15

World Carbon Dioxide Emissions from Fossil Fuels
billion metric tons

natural gas

oil

coal

1860 80 1900 20 40 60 80 88

Unhealthy Signs

Land—Our biological dependence on ecosystems is epitomized by our reliance on the earth's soil. A thin layer of topsoil provides food crops for more than 5 billion people and grazing for almost 4 billion domesticated animals. But that soil is vanishing: exposed by careless husbandry, it is carried away by the winds and rains. Each year, the world's farmers lose an estimated 24 billion tons of topsoil; during the past two decades, they have lost an amount of topsoil equal to that on India's cropland.

As the soil is eroded—or exhausted, paved over, or waterlogged and poisoned with salt by irrigation practices—the land loses its fertility. In its worst form, land degradation turns an estimated 6 million hectares worldwide to desert annually—an area nearly twice the size of Belgium lost beyond practical hope of reclamation. An area three times as large becomes so worn down each year that it is rendered unprofitable for farming and grazing.

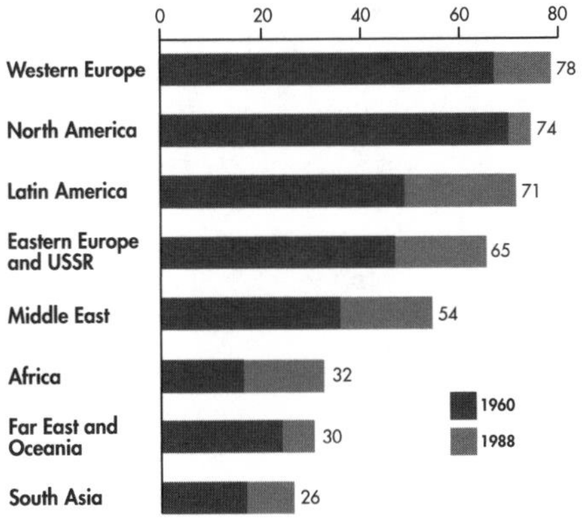

The silent scourge of land degradation is advancing almost everywhere soil is put to the plow. On every continent, between 27 and 62 percent of land is moderately to severely degraded—degraded to the point that potential crop yields are lowered by at least one-tenth.

Within that overall picture, irrigated lands—the most intensively cultivated of the world's lands—are especially degraded. Roughly one-third of the world's food is grown on the 17 percent of cropland that is irrigated, but over time, seepage from canals and overwatering of fields has caused the underlying water tables to rise. In the absence of adequate drainage, water eventually enters the root zone in a crop-damaging process called waterlogging. In dry regions, a process called salinization usually accompanies waterlogging: as moisture near the surface evaporates, it leaves behind a layer of salt that is toxic to plants. All told, harmful irrigation practices have lowered crop yields on about one-fourth of the world's irrigated area.

Cropland is also taken out of production by the encroachment of roads and cities. In the United States, 16 million hectares—more area than the entire state of Georgia—is now under pavement. As cities with near-stable populations in industrial countries sprawl across the landscape for lack of effective land-use plans, Third World cities explode with the influx of millions fleeing rural poverty. Since 1960 the urban population of the developing countries has increased from 22 percent to 33 percent of the total population (*chart 16*). Half of humanity is expected to live in cities shortly after the turn of the century, and most of the world's largest cities will be in the Third World.

All told, land degradation combined with other environmental problems such as air pollution may now be lowering world grain harvest by as much as one percent per year, offsetting roughly half of the nearly 2 percent per year gain from better farming methods. With population growing at 1.8 percent or 90 million per year, the world's farmers are pressed ever harder to keep food on the table.

Forests—If the world's soils have worn away gradually, the world's forests are suffering a frontal assault. Before the dawn of agriculture, some 10,000 years ago, the earth boasted a cloak of forest and open woodland covering some 6.2 billion hectares. Over the centuries, a combination of land clearing for crop production, commercial timber harvesting, and cattle ranching has shrunk the earth's forests to some 4.2 billion hectares. Forests in temperate lands were first to go, as the agricultural revolution and then the industrial revolution swept the northern hemisphere.

Since 1950, the loss of forests has shifted largely to the tropics. Ten tropical trees are cut for every one planted—in Africa the ratio is 29 to one—according to a global forest survey conducted a decade ago by the UN Food and Agriculture Organization (FAO). All told, FAO estimated that 11.3 million hectares of tropical forest are lost each year. More recent surveys, however, indicate that the old FAO figure is far too low. The World Resources Institute

CHART 16

Urban Population, 1960 and 1988

percent of total regional population

Region	Percent (1988)
Western Europe	78
North America	74
Latin America	71
Eastern Europe and USSR	65
Middle East	54
Africa	32
Far East and Oceania	30
South Asia	26

■ 1960
■ 1988

"Every year an area of forest equal to the whole surface of the United Kingdom is destroyed. At present rates (of clearance) we shall, by the year 2000, have removed 65 percent of forests in the humid tropical zones."
Margaret Thatcher
former Prime Minister, UK, 1989

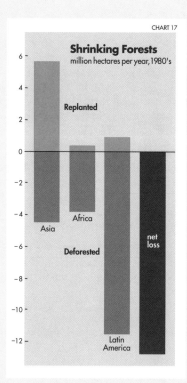

CHART 17

Shrinking Forests
million hectares per year, 1980's

Replanted

Asia

Africa

net loss

Deforested

Latin America

estimates the annual loss of tropical forests at between 13 and 20 million hectares. Assuming the high end of this range to be accurate, and subtracting all reported newly planted forests suggests an annual net loss of 12.6 million hectares of tropical forest area per year in the 1980s (*chart 17*).

Although tropical forests cover just 7 percent of the planet's land area, their importance to the biosphere is much greater. With warm, wet conditions nearly year-round, growing seasons never stop. Tropical forests serve as a gigantic storehouse for carbon. As whole tracts are cleared and burned, they release it as carbon dioxide into the atmosphere, where it traps heat, adding to global warming. Although ecologists cannot pinpoint the figures precisely, tropical deforestation overall probably contributes 14 percent of the greenhouse gases humanity releases each year (*chart 18, page 32*).

As the world's forests fall before waves of cattle ranchers, loggers, and dispossessed peasants, the patchy strips of woods and woodlots around farms have been carried away twig by twig to feed a billion family cookstoves. More than two-thirds of all Third World people, and nearly everyone in rural areas, rely on wood for cooking and heating. According to FAO, at least 1.2 billion people in developing countries are meeting their fuelwood needs only by cutting wood faster than it is being replaced. Nearly 100 million people—half of them in tropical Africa—cannot meet their minimum needs even by overcutting the woodlands around them.

When deforestation occurs on hillsides, soil and water follow the trees down the slope. Soil erosion fills rivers with sediment, traumatizing fisheries, clogging downstream irrigation works and hydroelectric facilities, and reducing the capacity of mountainous areas to absorb heavy rains. One consequence is worsened flooding, as in Bangladesh during the 1980s, partly due to the progressive deforestation of the Himalayan watershed. Early September 1988 found two-thirds of Bangladesh under water.

Living Species—Linked to the fate of the forests is the fate of evolution's masterwork: the profusion of living species that inhabit the tropics. The vast scale of the tropical rain forests, which cover an area larger than the continental United States, masks extraordinary biological diversity. Botanists from the Smithsonian Tropical Research Institute found 835 species of trees in one 50-hectare plot of Malaysian rain forest; an equivalent area of temperate forests might hold two dozen. Many tropical species have evolved to the point of living only in conjunction with one other species—the 900 varieties of fig trees, for instance, are each pollinated by a distinct species of wasp.

Rain forests are home to half of all species on earth, most of which are still undiscovered, unstudied, and unnamed. Biologists do not know whether humans share the earth with 3 million or 30 million living species, nor how many species have been lost already. It has been estimated that 10,000 species may be going extinct each year—about one per hour.

Many scientists believe that a larger share of the earth's plant and animal life will disappear in our lifetime than was lost in the mass extinction that included the disappearance of the dinosaurs 65 million years ago. It is likely to be the first time in evolution's stately course that plant communities, which anchor ecosystems and maintain the habitability of the earth, will also be devastated.

The loss of species, along with its ecological implications, foretells the loss of human lives, since tropical species are common sources of new medicines. One in four drugs comes from tropical forest plants, including the treatment for childhood leukemia. At least 1,400 tropical forest plants—and perhaps more than 10,000—have some effect against cancer; among them could be miracle drugs. We may never know.

The Military's Offensiv

In war—

What a war can do to the environment has been graphically revealed in the recent Persian Gulf War. Televised briefings reported "surgical strikes" and some "collateral damage." The reality was less antiseptic—hundreds of thousands of casualties and an ecological calamity: water and sewage systems and power networks widely destroyed; large oil spills in the Gulf, threatening the survival of wild life and the safety of water purification and power plants; hundreds of burning oil wells spreading soot and toxic chemicals as far as the Indian subcontinent.

Before that one, there were 227 other wars in this century, wreaking environmental damage in varying degrees. In Vietnam, one of the most fought-over regions in the world, the ecological devastation will take generations to repair. Between 1945 and 1975, the country's forest area fell by half; 15 million hectares were lost. The farm-land was pock-marked with 25 million bomb craters. To clear forests, US forces in the 1960's dropped 50 million liters of Agent Orange, a combination of herbicides. Forests and fisheries have not recovered; crop yields remain low. One-third of the country is considered wasteland. The population suffers an elevated incidence of birth defects, cancers, and other diseases.

And in peace—

Even in peacetime, military activities are particularly dangerous to the environment. For example, the process of creating and maintaining the world's stock of over 50,000 nuclear weapons is, as one US

Wastes—The global economy not only squanders forests, soils, and living species, it generates an enormous stream of waste products—garbage, toxic and radioactive chemicals, and pollutants of all types. Around the world, the introduction of the throwaway economy first identified with the United States has led to mountainous trash heaps. New York City, for example, discards 24,000 tons of solid wastes each day; the city's Fresh Kills landfill will soon be the highest point on the eastern seaboard south of Maine.

Equally troubling, the global waste steam is increasingly contaminated with compounds and chemicals that do not appear in nature—products that pose new and unknown threats to the environment and human health. Both the volume and the number of manufactured chemicals have burgeoned since World War II. In the United States, annual production of synthetic organic chemicals rose fifteenfold between 1945 and 1985, from 6.7 million metric tons to 102 million. Worldwide, some 70,000 chemicals are presently in everyday use, with between 500 and 1,000 new ones added to the list each year.

Among the most significant and dangerous of the synthetic chemicals are pesticides, whose use has skyrocketed worldwide since the 1960s. Pesticide use in the United States nearly tripled between 1965 and 1985. Since pesticides are spread widely over the land, they pose risks not only to farm workers but to the general population through residues in food crops and through contamination of drinking water.

Air—The era of cheap energy that began after World War II has had a particularly severe effect on the atmosphere, as fossil fuel combustion spews sulfur and nitrogen oxides, hydrocarbons, carbon monoxide, sooty "particulates" and countless minor pollutants into the air. And militarization, with its heavy use of fossil fuels, shares some of the blame for air pollution. The armed forces of former West Germany were estimated to account for 5 percent of nitrogen oxides, 4 percent of hydrocarbons, and 6 percent of carbon monoxide emitted in that nation. Including emissions from other NATO forces stationed in the former West Germany could double the shares, since their energy use matches that of the German military.

Air pollution-related health problems now span all continents and all levels of development. In greater Athens, the number of deaths rises sixfold on heavily polluted days. In Hungary, the National Institute of Public Health reports that every seventeenth death is caused by air pollution. And in Bombay, breathing the air is equivalent to smoking 10 cigarettes a day.

The environmental impacts of air pollution are equally grave. The tall smokestacks that were built in the 1960s and 1970s to disperse emissions became conduits to the upper atmosphere for sulfur dioxide and nitrogen oxides, which, through chemical reactions, become acid rain.

Acid rain's effects on bodies of water were recognized first in Scandinavia, where aquatic life in thousands of lakes has died. Fish in Norwegian lakes have died off in an area of water covering 13,000 square kilometers. In eastern Canada, 150,000 lakes suffer some biological damage from acid rain, while the United States has about 1,000 acidified lakes. Four percent of streams in the mid-Atlantic region of the United States are similarly affected, and half of all streams are susceptible to acidification because of their limited ability to neutralize acid. The threat to coastal waters may be of similar magnitude. A 1988 study by the Environmental Defense Fund concluded that acid deposition is a major contributor to the degradation of the Chesapeake Bay.

In the early 1980s, concern about the effects of acid deposition spread from water to land. Signs of widespread forest damage attributable to acid deposition combined with air pollution first arose in West Germany. The share of forests there showing signs of damage rose from 8 percent in 1982, the first year a survey was done, to 54 percent in 1986, and has since declined slightly to 52 percent in 1988—partly because trees already dead are not counted in each new survey. Across Europe, nearly 50 million hectares have been damaged by the combined effects of acid rain and air pollution, representing 35 percent of Europe's total forested area.

Ozone Layer—Pollutants rising into the upper atmosphere are having a similarly destructive effect on the invisible layer of ozone, a form of oxygen, that prevents harmful solar ultraviolet radiation from reaching the surface of the earth. Since 1979, a hole in the ozone layer over Antarctica has been opening each spring.

Damage is not limited to the south pole. Between 1969 and 1986, the average global concentration of ozone in the stratosphere fell about 2 percent. The magnitude of the decline varied, with the most heavily populated regions of Europe, North America, and the Soviet Union suffering a year-round depletion of 3 percent and a winter loss of 5 percent.

As ozone diminishes in the upper atmosphere, the earth receives more ultraviolet radiation, and even small losses of ozone can have severe health and environmental impacts. Reduced crop yields, depleted marine fisheries, materials damage, and increased smog are also results of higher levels of radiation.

gainst the Environment

General Accounting Office report put it, "one of the more potentially dangerous industrial operations in the world."

Not only does nuclear weapons production involve the intricate manipulation and transportation of enormous quantities of radioactive materials, it also creates great volumes of non-radioactive hazardous wastes. And because all operations are carried out under strict secrecy, civilian environmental agencies and citizen watchdog groups are kept in the dark. All indications are that military enterprises are also the least regulated hazardous industries in the world.

Because of the extensive military use of electronics and fire extinguishers, the ozone damage of military endeavors is massive. The US Defense Department, for example, accounts for 76 percent of emissions of a type of halon called halon-1211, and nearly half the emissions of the form of CFC called CFC-113. Halons in most civilian fire extinguishers are never released to the atmosphere because they are never used. But US military regulations require that every tank's fire-fighting equipment be tested *with* halons; no substitutes are allowed. Other nations' armies undoubtedly have similar procedures.

Militarization has a black mark for its greenhouse record too. In 1988, the US military consumed an estimated 1,589 trillion BTUs of energy—86 percent of all US government energy use and about 14 times the energy used by all urban public and private mass transit in America. The total carbon emissions of the world's combined military forces is probably on the order of 140 million tons, nearly equal to the annual emissions of the United Kingdom. Including energy consumption by weapons industries could well double the total.

CHART 18

Sources of Global Warming

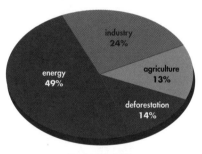

CFC's
20%

methane
16%

carbon dixiode
50%

8%

6%

tropospheric
ozone

nitrous oxide

Greenhouse Gases

industry
24%

energy
49%

agriculture
13%

deforestation
14%

Human Activities

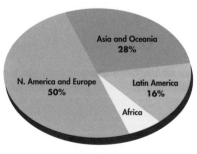

Asia and Oceania
28%

N. America and Europe
50%

Latin America
16%

Africa

Regional Emissions

Where the harm ends no one knows—the ozone layer has been intact since before life on land began.

Compounds containing chlorine and bromine, which are released from industrial processes and products and then move slowly into the upper atmosphere, are the primary culprits. Most of the chlorine comes from chlorofluorocarbons (CFCs)—common industrial chemicals used as coolants in refrigerators and air conditioners, as propellants in some aerosol sprays, and as cleaning agents in the manufacture of electronic devices. The bromine originates from halons used in fire extinguishers.

Climate—All the maladies afflicting the planet are serious, but the most dangerous of all is the threat of catastrophic climate change due to the invisible accumulation of heat-trapping greenhouse gases in the atmosphere. The chemical composition of the earth's atmosphere, normally stable for millennia, has been substantially altered over the past century and a half. Carbon dioxide concentration is up 25 percent, nitrous oxide 19 percent, and methane 100 percent. To complicate matters further, CFCs, besides depleting the ozone layer also trap heat, adding further to this warm blanket of gases that allows sunlight in but holds in the resulting heat.

Global average temperatures are now about 0.6 degrees Celsius warmer than they were a century ago. As yet, no conclusive proof links this recent heating to global warming, but circumstantial evidence has convinced many scientists nonetheless. Scientists are more concerned, however, about the much faster warming that is predicted by a half dozen computer models—reaching 2.5–5.5 degrees Celsius late in the next century. Severe tropical storms, droughts, heat waves, crop failures, and floods are all likely to be much more common in a greenhouse world.

World agriculture is particularly vulnerable to climate change. Most climate models predict that the major grain growing regions of North America and central China will become substantially hotter and drier, forcing some farmers to switch to lower-yielding dryland crops and forcing others out of production.

Biological diversity, already endangered by loss of forest habitat, is another likely casualty of global warming. As climate zones shift suddenly, whole ecosystems could be trapped in climates they cannot adapt to quickly enough. Forests, wetlands, and even the polar tundra could be irrevocably damaged.

Sea level rise is another threat. As the water in the ocean warms and as water trapped in glaciers and ice caps begins to melt more rapidly, oceans will expand. By the end of the next century, the seas may be up by 1-2 meters, inundating large areas of wetland that nourish the world's fisheries and threatening many coastal cities. Protecting the entire US east coast could cost more than $300 billion by 2100, according to the EPA.

Few countries can afford such investment. Most at risk are Third World countries, particularly in Asia, where millions of people live and farm on river deltas and flood plains. In Bangladesh, sea level rise and subsidence caused by human activities could flood up to 18 percent of the nation's land area by 2050, displacing over 17 million people. And this change might not be incremental. Millions of lives could be lost in a matter of days when tropical storms overwhelm areas that have been getting gradually closer to the sea.

The world energy system is directly responsible for half of the human-released greenhouse gases, adding not only 5.9 billion tons of carbon to the atmosphere in the form of carbon dioxide annually but substantial quantities of two other important gases as well—methane and nitrous oxide (*chart 18*). Carbon-containing fossil fuels provide almost four-fifths of the world's energy, and their use continues to grow 3 percent annually. Overall, the fifth of humanity living in North America and Europe is responsible for about half of the problem. The rich industrial countries have caused most of the damage to the global atmosphere so far, and thus have a clear responsibility to take the lead in formulating solutions.

Environmental Protection

Win Some

• Thailand banned logging permits in 1988, outlawing the timber industry which had cut back Thailand's forest cover from two-thirds to one-third of its land.

• Brazil's fertility rate (number of children per mother) has declined from 5.7 to about 3.4 today, one of the fastest rates of decline in the world.

• The World Bank plans a three-fold increase in funding for family planning over the next three years.

• More than 90 nations agreed in June 1990 to halt CFC production by the turn of the century.

• At least 14 countries plan to complete the phase-out of CFC's before 2000.

• A government-sponsored salinity program in Australia is conducting a tree planting campaign to halt salt build-up on a million acres of prime farmland.

• Czechoslovakia will defer mining a recently discovered huge gold deposit until completion of a study of the environmental impact of mining in the area.

• Britain has abandoned its pursuit of nuclear energy and the USSR has closed or cancelled at least 30 nuclear reactors since the Chernobyl accident in 1988.

• The European Parliament elections in 1989 doubled the number of Green Party delegates to 39.

Lose Some

• Burma's sales of logging concessions to Thai companies are helping to finance its military campaigns; 1.2 million acres of Burma's forests disappear yearly.

• Nigeria, India, and Egypt, which together have nearly one-fifth of the world's people, have failed to control population growth.

• The US continues to deny funding for the UN Population Fund; 37 of the world's poorest countries have had to cut family planning programs for lack of funds.

• Even if CFC's are phased out by the year 2000, an estimated 20 billion pounds of ozone-depleting chemicals will be emitted over the next 25 years.

• Salt accumulation is reducing yields on 24 percent of world irrigated land. Each year the world's farmers lose an estimated 24 billion tons of topsoil.

• With the air in Mexico City at more than three times the maximum acceptable ozone level, the authorities declared a pollution emergency, forcing an industrial slowdown.

• Japan plans to recover plutonium from its reactor wastes and over the next 30 years to ship from Europe as much as 150 tons of this highly toxic substance to use as fuel in its nuclear power plants.

• The state of Amazonas, Brazil, which contains an area of rain forest almost three times the size of France, elected a governor strongly opposed to environmental protection.

Remedies

A global action plan for restoring the health of the planet is needed to lay out the priorities for action against land degradation, loss of forests and biological diversity, the swelling global waste stream, and the atmospheric perils of air pollution, acid rain, ozone depletion, and climate change. Among the numerous policies and initiatives that could help address these menaces, a handful are central: slowing population growth, reducing global inequity, reforesting the earth, and weaning societies from their reliance on fossil fuels.

Slowing Population Growth—Population stabilization is the only acceptable goal in a world where growth in human numbers is leading to a life-threatening deterioration of environmental systems. In 13 countries, home to some 266 million people, birth rates have already fallen to the point where births and deaths are in balance. The world's remaining nations, on the other hand, are far from the goal. In much of Africa the population growth rate hovers around 3 percent per year.

At this point, the only socially-responsible step for the United Nations, the World Bank, and the international development community is to call for—and provide the funds to implement—a sharp reduction in the world population growth rate. Recent surveys in developing countries indicate that approximately one-third of women wish to limit family size but lack access to family planning services.

Providing contraceptives alone is inadequate to the goal of dramatically reducing population growth rates. Women have fewer children only when those children survive—making universal primary health care a critical component—and when women are armed with information and skills that raise their status in society. Universal female literacy is thus a second indispensable part of any population stabilization strategy.

Reducing Global Inequity—Realistically, it will be impossible to slow population growth so long as Third World nations are getting poorer by the year, as many have been in the past decade. Forty-three so-called developing nations might better have been called disintegrating nations since the international debt crisis began in the early 1980s. Fourteen of them have seen their per capita income decline as much since their troubles began as did the United States during the Great Depression. At the global level, the net effect of Third World debt is simple but devastating: it requires the transfer of $50 billion dollars from poor nations to rich ones each year.

Global inequity is deeper than the debt crisis, with roots in local and international economies, including everything from patterns of trade to rising landlessness. Despite steady economic growth in the world economy over the past decade, the poor have increased in number by more than 200 million. Today 1.2 billion people live beneath the threshold of basic needs. The gap dividing the rich from the poor has never been wider: the top fifth of the population on the global economic ladder enjoys 60 times the goods and services of the lowest fifth.

This rising poverty is bound up with environmental deterioration as well, as people desperate to feed their children put rain forests to the torch and steep slopes to the plow. In broad regions of the world, the poor are caught in a downward spiral of economic and ecological decline; they are forced to sacrifice the environment to save their lives.

Reducing the Third World's $1.2 trillion debt to the industrial countries to a point where social progress can begin again would be a first step toward a global pattern of development that puts the poor and their environments first. Also important are reforms in development policies at the national and international levels to make official agencies work effectively with the hundreds of thousands of grassroots self-help organizations that the poor have formed over the past three decades. Sustainable development can come only with progress from the bottom and the top simultaneously.

Reforesting the Earth—Vigorous efforts to protect remaining tropical forests and to plant several billion more trees each year is a third action priority. It is critical for protecting species, spoils, and meeting human needs; it is also an important way to limit climate change, since trees pull carbon out of the atmosphere.

Many tropical countries—plagued by debt, weak economies, and burgeoning populations—see few alternatives to clearing forests as ways to earn quick foreign exchange, to spur regional development, or to open up new areas for settlement. They continue to promote wasteful and destructive logging and the clearing of primary forest for cropping and grazing, even though such activities are not economically or ecologically sustainable. Much forest has been cleared in Brazil, for example, because of government subsidies that encourage cattle ranching, even though depletion of the pastureland's fertility causes the ventures to be abandoned in a matter of years. International support for popular organizations native to forest regions—such as Indian tribes—can strengthen their standing enough to safeguard forests.

A major global reforestation effort is the other key component of a strategy to preserve and expand the world's forest cover. Trees need to be planted on the equivalent of 130 million hectares—an area slightly larger than Ethiopia—in order to meet growing demands for fuelwood and industrial wood products and to stabilize soil and water resources in the Third World. Accomplishing this goal over the next 15 years would require planting some 15 billion trees annually.

Examples of the diverse kinds of reforestation needed already exist. In Kenya, the Greenbelt Movement, sponsored by the National Council of Women, has mobilized more than 15,000 farmers and a half million schoolchildren in planting more than 10 million trees. And the American Forestry Association has initiated an urban reforestation program with a target of planting some 100 million trees in cities and suburbs around the US by 1992.

Weaning Ourselves from Fossil Fuels—The fourth priority for action is making a transition away from fossil fuel-based energy systems—in order to reduce air pollution, acid rain, and the emissions of greenhouse gases. The centerpiece of any workable attempt to do this is to improve energy efficiency. Improved energy efficiency can have a large and immediate impact on carbon emissions. For example, the efficiency of US buildings, industry, and transportation improved 26 percent between 1973 and 1987; this kept US carbon emissions at 1.2 billion tons instead of 1.6 billion tons annually. An additional output of 300 million tons of carbon emissions was avoided by efficiency improvements in other countries. Similar gains are possible in the future

Shifting to more fuel-efficient transportation can sharply reduce carbon emissions. The world's nearly 400 million cars currently spew some 700 million tons of carbon into the atmosphere each year, 13 percent of the total from fossil fuels. Projection based on recent trends would have these emissions nearly doubling by 2010. However, if a combination of improved mass transit, greater use of bicycles for short trips, and a tax on carbon-emitting fuels kept the world fleet to 500 million cars by the year 2010, and if these vehicles averaged 50 miles to the gallon rather than the current 20, automobile carbon emissions would fall to half of what they are today.

Carbon emissions can also be lowered by improving the efficiency of electricity-using devices. Some 64 percent of the world's electricity is generated using fossil fuels (chiefly coal), accounting for 27 percent of global carbon emissions from fossil fuels. Electricity is used in many different ways, all of which can become far more efficient. Based on current technologies, for example, electric motors can be made at least 40 percent more efficient than they are today, and lighting systems 75 percent more efficient.

Finally, overall energy efficiency can be greatly increased by moving away from the throwaway pattern of materials use that is now predominant. Reemphasizing durability, reuse, and recyling could save enormous amounts of energy. The energy thrown out with the trash is a colossal waste. Aluminum recyling saves 95 percent of the energy used in aluminum manufacturing; steel and paper recycling save up to three quarters, and glass saves up to a third. Recyling also reduces air and water pollution, mining wastes and water consumption, not to mention reducing needs for landfills or incinerators.

Renewable sources of energy have a smaller immediate potential in displacing fossil fuels than energy efficiency improvements do. However, that potential will grow as the technologies are improved. The outlines of a successful strategy already exist. Solar, hydro, wind, and geothermal power have been pursued with notable success by governments and private companies since the mid-seventies. Across a broad spectrum of technologies, costs have fallen steadily and performance has improved. If renewable sources are to supply a large share of the world's energy by mid-century, then they must be vigorously developed today.

•••••

Human activities have pushed the planet's natural support systems dangerously out of kilter. Continuing on a business-as-usual path thus virtually assures severe economic disruption, social instability, and human suffering. In these last few years of the twentieth century, difficult questions of social equity, national sovereignty, and individual rights and responsibilities are emerging. A person may be able to afford a large-energy-consumptive automobile, but can the planet afford it? Similarly, a couple may desire and be able to support several children, but can the planet afford several children per family?

Like it or not, we find ourselves in a world where we are responsible for each other's well-being. Inefficient use of fossil fuels in the Soviet Union and the United States contributes to global warming and thus to the eventual inundation of rich cropland in the Nile River delta of Egypt. Uncontrolled air pollution by any country in central Europe threatens forests throughout the region. The use of CFCs anywhere puts the ozone layer at risk everywhere. There is no substitute for global solutions, based on international goals.

If the momentum for improved relations between West and East since mid-century can be maintained, the time may be near when the world's major powers make peace with each other in order to make peace with the earth. The arms race that has been the center of international affairs these past decades has been essentially a process by which we have pillaged our houses to build walls around them. We are left, sadly, with impressive walls and an impoverished home—a planet with poisoned air, water, and soil, with worn farms, denuded hillsides, and with fewer species living each hour.

Agreements to Safeguard the Environment*

Proposals to guard natural resources through treaties date back to 1872, when Switzerland called on its neighbors to join in creating a Europe-wide body to protect nesting sites of migratory birds. Switzerland was a century ahead of its time: the 1970s saw the first major round of global accords, with agreements covering everything from trade in leopard pelts to disposal of wastes on the high seas. A second round of major advances starting in the mid-1980s led to breakthrough agreements on ozone layer protection at Montreal and London, and the global waste trade at Basel.

On paper, the record of international agreements for protection of the global resources looks impressive. In practice, it has been feeble, hampered above all by an almost complete lack of effective international enforcement mechanisms. Jealous of their sovereignty, few states are willing to back up their official commitment to high-minded goals by empowering larger bodies with real authority. Even the Basel Convention on traffic in hazardous materials, a fairly simple agreement to monitor, has few teeth.

All of these international accords, on the other hand, are steps in the right direction. The critical question is whether leaders come to see quickly enough that their nations' true interests lie in strong, enforceable international standards. Without such overarching regulation, national attempts to address environmental decline will be fragmentary and piecemeal.

What promises to be the most difficult and most crucial environmental issue is still to be dealt with at the international level: global warming. The challenge is fundamental, involving fuels, industrial processes, and land use patterns that are embedded in conventional notions of human progress. No states can be left out of an agreement; though rich countries have done most of the damage to date, poor ones' emissions are rising far faster (*charts 19* and *20*).

To Protect Species and Preserve Critical Ecosystems

Wetlands (Ramsar), 1971   **61 states[1]**
Protects designated wetlands from encroachment, particularly those important for migrating birds, through an international registry.

World Heritage, 1972   **113 states[1]**
Protects cultural and natural heritage sites of outstanding universal value.

Endangered Species, 1973   **108 states[1]**
Limits international trade in endangered flora and fauna, or in products made from them, through a tight system of import-export permits.

To Protect the Marine Environment

Ocean Dumping, 1972   **70 states[2]**
Controls marine pollution by banning dumping of harmful substances and limiting dumping of others, and by establishing an international mechanism to adjudicate disputes.

Ship Pollution, 1978   **51 states[2]**
Reduces risk of pollution by oil and other harmful substances.

Law of the Sea, 1982   **45 states[3]**
Establishes a comprehensive legal regime for oceans and seas; sets environmental standards and enforcement provisions to control marine pollution.

To Control Substances Dangerous to Nature or Human Health

Protection of the Ozone Layer, 1985   **57 States[2]**
The Vienna Convention calls for collaborative research and careful monitoring of ozone layer to protect human health and the environment. This agreement set the stage for aggressive CFC control two years later.

Substances that Deplete the Ozone Layer, 1987   **58 states[2]**
The Montreal Protocol requires a 50 percent reduction in production of chlorofluorcarbons (CFC's) by 1999. Marked first major step on a global ecological threat.

CFC Control, 1990   **93 states[2]**
The London Meeting amends the Montreal Protocol, calling for a phase-out of CFC's by 2000, with extensions for developing countries.

Hazardous Waste Movement, 1989   **41 states[2]**
The Basel Convention restricts international traffic in hazardous materials, particularly export of toxics from rich to poor states.

*Selected agreements, global in scope; see also page 44
1. Number of ratifications as recorded by Westing Associates, Putney, VT, USA as of January 1991.
2. Number of states signing; they may or may not have ratified.
3. Number of ratifications; not yet in force (for which 60 ratifying states are needed).

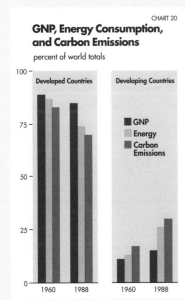

CHART 19

Carbon Dixode Emissions Projected*
billion tons

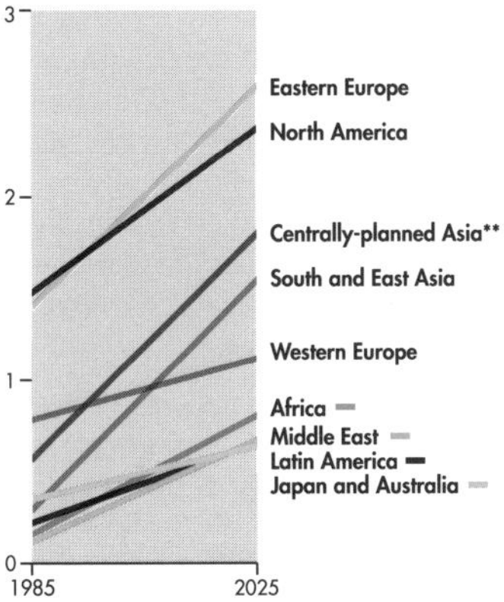

Eastern Europe
North America
Centrally-planned Asia**
South and East Asia
Western Europe
Africa
Middle East
Latin America
Japan and Australia

1985   2025

*Projections assume no specific international agreement to reduce emissions
**Cambodia, China, North Korea, Laos, Vietnam

CHART 20

GNP, Energy Consumption, and Carbon Emissions
percent of world totals

Developed Countries   Developing Countries

■ GNP
■ Energy
■ Carbon Emissions

1960   1988   1960   1988

Environment and Health

In the 4th century B.C., Hippocrates identified a case of lead poisoning, the first recognized occupational disease. In the late 18th century, Sir Percivall Pott linked the high incidence of scrotal cancer in chimney sweeps to their heavy exposure to soot. Since then, humanity's knowledge, as well as its continued use and abuse of the earth's natural resources, have exposed an astonishing array of links between the environment and human health.

Human assaults on the planet, all in the name of progress—harnessing energy, plumbing the earth's depths, manipulating plants and animals—are creating a multitude of health perils. The earth will survive this tampering; it is, after all, some 4.5 billion years old, and man merely a recent arrival. But human lives are endangered daily by tainted air and soil, and by polluted water traceable to human actions. Gases released by industry are eroding the earth's stratospheric ozone layer, permitting harmful solar rays to reach unwary populations. The same gases trap the sun's heat and affect global climate, encouraging a greenhouse effect. A gradual warming of the globe might, in time, bring about climate changes that could endanger the human race.

How ironic that a century which can justly pride itself on scientific prowess and on tangible improvements in public health is also capable of self-inflicted health damage. Worldwide, life expectancy has risen steadily, yet at the same time the toll of human lives attributable to human folly is also rising. On one side of the scale: life-saving medications, growing control of virulent diseases, new methods for improving water quality, breakthroughs in genetic engineering; on the other side, polluted air, toxic substances, shortages of food, vanishing forests, depleted soil, the time bomb of continuing population expansion (*chart 21*), and the specters of poverty and disease.

Some sobering figures reveal the extent of man's inhumanity to man:

- Four out of five cancers are linked to environmental causes, direct or indirect.

- Diarrheal diseases kill over 1,000 children every hour.

- Pesticides are causing 1 million severe-to-acute human poisonings a year.

- About 80 percent of all sickness and disease in the world is attributable, directly or indirectly, to unsafe water and sanitation.

- An estimated 625 million people are exposed to unhealthy levels of sulfur dioxide; more than 1 billion to excess levels of particles from acid rain.

- Worldwide, 2.4 billion pounds of hazardous pollutants, including toxic chemicals that cause cancer and harm the nervous system, are emitted yearly.

The actual toll of human suffering from environmentally-related health damage is far greater than this partial list suggests. The genesis of certain illnesses can be hard to document. Reports from developing countries are often incomplete. Another complicating element is time: for example, it may take 20 to 40 years of exposure to cancer-causing substances before the cancers which result from them can be detected. In many cases, governments have not collected data on activities under their control, or are reluctant to provide documentation; this hampers research, particularly in the nuclear field.

There is growing public awareness of the potential health dangers from abuse to the environment. In the US, the Environmental Protection Agency (EPA) has ranked air pollution, indoor and outdoor, as the top health hazard; next comes the exposure of workers to toxic chemicals, followed closely by the pollution of drinking water. Somewhat lower on the risk scale: the hazards posed by herbicides and pesticides; surface water contamination; acid depositions in air and water; and airborne toxic substances. The dangers of ground pollution, including hazardous wastes, and the escape of radioactive materials, serious as they are, were lower in their ranking. For the developing world, the sequence of leading perils may be somewhat different, since their most immediate problems are water-related. Less directly linked to immediate health problems, but judged most threatening of all is the prospect of global warming, now acknowledged as a major ecological risk whose consequences could be cataclysmic.

Prepared by **Arlette Brauer,** Contributing Editor of *MD* magazine, and Editor, *The Modern Medical Encyclopedia.* Mrs. Brauer was author of *The State of World Health* in *WMSE 1989.*

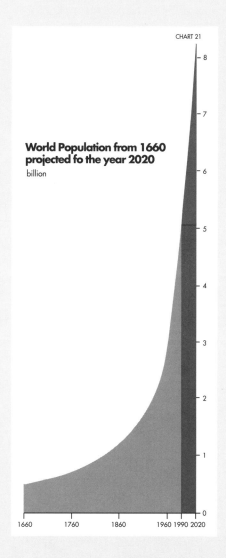

"Human concern with the environment must be focused on human health and well-being, for man is at one and the same time the prime source of environmental degradation and its prime victim."

Dr. Mostafa Kamal Tolba
Egypt, 1978

CHART 21

World Population from 1660 projected fo the year 2020

billion

8
7
6
5
4
3
2
1
0

1660   1760   1860   1960 1990 2020

Population pressure—The assault on world resources and the harm to health that follow result in large part from rapid population growth. Although some progress has been made in curbing the rate of growth, the hard truth is that more than 90 million people are added to the world's numbers each year, and more than 90 percent of them live in developing countries, where living conditions are all too often harsh. World population is now over 5 billion, and is expected to exceed 6 billion by the year 2000, 10 billion by 2025 (*chart 21*).

In urban areas of the industralized world—and increasingly in the developing world—population crowding and high levels of energy use breed foul air, water, and soil. In Third World cities, rampant pollution fosters the spread of typhoid fever, cholera, and hepatitis.

Slowing population growth is an effective way to improve the lives of people today and in the future. In the developing world, some 100 million couples who would like to limit family size do not have the means to do so. Only four of the world's 170 countries limit access to family planning, but the needs far outstrip available services.

Funding is a problem. Family planning has commanded only a very modest share of government budgets in developing countries, and no more than 1 percent of all funds available through official development assistance. These sums will clearly not meet the challenges of the future. UN estimates that it would cost $9 billion to supply family planning services to 570 million couples wanting those services by the end of the decade. To meet these needs, support through international programs must reach $4.5 billion yearly by 2000, a 7-fold increase over present levels of annual assistance.

Educating women is a lifeline to better health. It gives them the opportunity to make informed choices in both planning and caring for their families. Globally, one woman in three is illiterate as compared to one man in five—simply because young girls do not have the access to schools that boys do. The relationship between a mother's education and the number of children she bears is clear. The contrasts are striking (*chart 22*). In Latin America, where the difference is most extreme, mothers who have 7 or more years of education average half as many children as uneducated mothers—four less per mother.

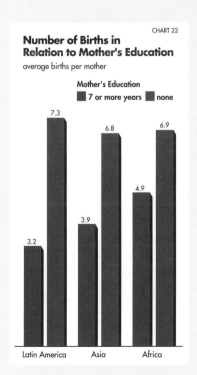

CHART 22

Number of Births in Relation to Mother's Education

average births per mother

Mother's Education
■ 7 or more years ■ none

Latin America: 3.2, 7.3
Asia: 3.9, 6.8
Africa: 4.9, 6.9

Environmental Damage and its Toll

Air Pollution—One-fifth of humanity lives in areas where the air is unfit to breathe. Although some progress in clearing the air has been made in the last decade, the juggernaut of industrial growth rolls on relentlessly, spreading increasing quantities of dangerous substances into the atmosphere, shrouding crowded cities with a visible pall. Contaminants from the burning of fossil fuels billow from smokestacks, from home furnaces, from the tailpipes of growing swarms of motor vehicles. In the US alone, 107 million kilograms of carcinogens were released by industry in 1987.

Airborne pollutants increase the frequency with which people, especially children and the elderly, develop respiratory ailments; they also heighten the severity of the illness. The human body absorbs gases and particulates—fine particles of dust and soot—into the bloodstream. They cause serious damage to the lungs and to the respiratory tract, impair the ability of the blood to carry oxygen, affect the nervous and cardiovascular system, and foster eye irritation. Some of the substances can trigger gene mutations, birth defects, and cancer (*table,* page 38).

The major pollutants currently defiling the atmosphere are toxic gases, particulates, and lead. When some of these pollutants react with oxygen in the presence of sunlight, they produce ground-level ozone, which inflames lung tissue, constricting the bronchial system and forcing the body to work harder to keep oxygen flowing through the blood. Ozone is also a major contributor to smog, plague of major cities around the world. Recent studies show that far lower levels of smog than previously believed can trigger breathing problems and inflict long-term damage even in vigorous adults in good health.

Acid precipitation, another airborne bane, is an international problem that mainly afflicts developed countries. The acid rain falls to the earth, often miles away from its original source; it leaches such toxic metals as lead and mercury from the soil into streams and ground water tables, injuring human health as well as entire fish populations.

Because people spend an estimated 80 percent of their time at home, health hazards from indoor pollution can also be grave. Many pollutants occur in more concentrated form in an enclosed area, both in the work place and in the house, and can often exceed acceptable health limits: nitrogen oxides and carbon dioxide from gas stove and heaters, auto exhausts in attached garages, particles of soot, benzopyrene from tobacco smoking. Formaldehyde fumes rise from pressed wood products, permanent press fabrics, and glue. Other volatile compounds lurk in familiar products—in paints, solvents, aerosol sprays, moth repellents, air fresheners.

One of the most notorious of indoor pollutants is asbestos, particularly in developed countries. It was widely used in buildings until the 1960s before science learned that inhaling its fibers could cause cancer and asbestosis. The traditional fuels, mainly firewood, which is widely used for cooking and heating water, are an important though neglected health menace throughout the Third World. Perhaps 80 percent of global exposure to air pollution by particulates occurs indoors in developing countries. The smoke from primitive stoves distributes large quantities of benzopyrene and other dangerous hydrocarbons. The effects are largely borne by women who do the cooking, and by their small children.

Hazardous Substances and Wastes—Less ubiquitous than some air pollutants, but insidiously harmful, hazardous substances are recognized as a major health threat. Industrial chemicals, metals, pesticides, toxic wastes, including dangerous nuclear debris, intrude into homes and work places. In growing quantities, they pollute the air, the soil, and the water supply, and many of them remain a major disposal problem after use.

The health damage from hazardous substances (by definition, carcinogenic and toxic, corrosive and ignitable) can come from direct

Environmental Illnesses

Human health is in jeopardy because of man-made changes in the environment in the name of progress. The roster of illnesses directly or indirectly related to environmental damage is deplorably long; the list below merely suggests the wide range of both chronic and acute health problems induced by contaminants introduced into the air, water, and soil of our planet.

Although some pollutants are more commonly found in air than in soil or water, many can move freely from one medium to another. Toxic wastes in leaking landfills can contaminate both surface and ground water, and enter the food chain; toxic fumes escape into the air through incineration. Some toxic substances penetrate the skin. Deposits of acid rain foul land and water.

Hazardous Substances

Substance*	Source	Health Effects
Benzene	Solvents, pharmaceuticals, detergent production.	Cancer, leukemia, nausea, loss of muscle coordination, bone marrow damage.
Cadmium	Batteries, zinc and fertilizer processing.	Damage to liver and kidneys, anemia, gastro-intestinal problems.
Lead[3]	Paint, gasoline, solder.	Neurotoxic; may cause mental impairment in children; affects brain, kidneys, other organs.
Mercury, nickel, other heavy metals	House paint, electroplating, laboratories.	Brain damage, possible lung cancer, respiratory problems, lesions, kidney failure.
PCBs	Electronics, hydraulic fluid, fluorescent lights.	Skin damage, possible skin cancer, birth defects, gastro-intestinal damage, reproductive failures.
Vinyl chloride[3]	Plastics production.	Kidney, lung, and liver cancer; may harm fetuses.

Water Pollutants

BHC	Insecticides.	Possible cancer, embryo damage.
Chlorinated solvents	Chemical production and degreasing, machinery upkeep.	Possible cancer.
DDT	Insecticides.	Possible cancer, liver damage, embryo damage.
Parasites and insects	Land runoffs and flooding.	Malaria, filariasis, river blindness, schistosomiasis, other tropical ills.
Pathogenic bacteria and viruses	Leaking septic tanks, untreated sewage.	Gastro-intestinal illnesses, typhoid, cholera, hepatitis, eye diseases.
Trihalomethane	Chemical reaction in chlorinated water.	Damage to kidneys and liver, possible cancer.

Airborne Pollutants

Asbestos[3]	Deteriorated insulation or fire-proofing.	Cancer and lung diseases.
Carbon dioxide[1]	Combustion of oil, coal, natural gas, deforestation.	Angina and other serious heart problems.
Carbon monoxide	Motor vehicles, fossil fuel combustion, mines.	Blocks blood absorption of oxygen; drowsiness; can cause unconsciousness and death.
CFCs and halons	Refrigerants, foams, aerosols, solvents.	Ultraviolet radiation, causing skin cancer, eye disorders.
Formaldehyde[3]	Bonding agent in plywood, used in building, furniture.	Irritates eyes, nose, and throat; causes rashes, allergic reactions; possible carcinogen.
Ground-level ozone[1]	Principal constituent of smog.	Impairs breathing; aggravates lung and heart disease.
Hydrocarbons	Motor vehicles, industry.	Some types carcinogenic or toxic.
Nitrogen oxides[1,2]	Power plants, motor vehicles.	Lung irritation; enhance susceptibility to viral infections.
Particulates (soot, smoke, etc.)	Power plants, industry, motor vehicles.	Lung and eye irritation; respiratory disorders.
Sulfur dioxide[2]	Power plants.	Respiratory diseases, eye irritation.
Radio nuclides	Nuclear plants.	Lung, bone cancer; kidney damage.

*See page 61 for definitions of terms.
[1]Contributes to global warming [2]Causes acid rain [3]Primarily indoor hazards

contact or from contaminated air and water. Depending on the substance and the degree of exposure, problems vary from acute topical effects like skin burns and rashes or lung irritation, to more serious, chronic illnesses with a longer latency period—cancer, brain damage, nerve and digestive disorders, and reproductive troubles. Of the 70,000 chemicals now used regularly, little is known about the health effects of four-fifths of them, but a great number are suspect.

Some 35 heavy metals are dangerous to humans. As particulate emissions or as contaminants of food and water, they can cause rashes and ulceration, or accumulate in the brain, liver, or kidneys, with fatal results. Repeated exposure to lead can cause grave, long-term damage. It builds up in bones and soft tissues, affects the blood-forming organs, the kidneys, and the nervous system. Lead poisoning has been singled out as the leading environmental health problem for America's children. The greatest hazard comes from lead paint. Even at low levels of exposure, lead is dangerous because it can impair neurological development and lower ability to learn. Experts estimate that in the US alone, close to 17 percent of all urban children—and two-thirds of all black inner-city children—have been affected by excessive levels of lead. In Mexico City, 7 out of 10 newborns were reported to have lead levels above WHO norms, suggesting that an entire generation of children may be intellectually impaired.

Press reports of a ship that roamed the oceans for more than two years in search of a dumping ground for 13,000 tons of waste have helped to dramatize the increasing problems of waste disposal. Improper storage and disposal of hazardous wastes are growing dangers. If these wastes are placed in plain metal drums that can corrode, or if they are dumped in unlined ponds or landfills, they may leach out into the nearby soil or water supply. Emissions from waste stored above the ground can mix with the air and affect those living or working downwind from the site. Some components of highly radioactive and extremely toxic wastes from nuclear and chemical weapons sites remain lethal for hundreds, even thousands of years.

As landfill space becomes scarce, disposal problems multiply. The opening in New Mexico of the first US permanent nuclear waste repository, designed to seal plutonium wastes in a jacket of solid salt, has been delayed by legislative disputes. Opponents describe it as an $800 million tomb under the desert.

Pesticides—Hailed at first as miracle workers protecting crops from disease and insect damage, pesticides are now losing their prestige. Not only are some of them less effective, but potent ones have been declared hazardous to health. They contaminate water in rural areas, taint the food crops they are meant to protect, and pollute the atmosphere. Yet their use is increasing 12 percent yearly worldwide, and will undoubtedly continue to do so since expanding populations demand ever greater food supplies.

The toll of pesticide poisoning is sobering: between 400,000 and 2,000,000 people are affected yearly worldwide; many of these are acute poisonings and 14,000 to 40,000 die yearly. Many of these deaths occur in developing countries, where farmers are less likely to take proper precautions. Third World nations use only 10 to 25 percent of the world's production of pesticides, but suffer up to 50 percent of the acute poisonings, in part because of illiteracy, but also because of limited access to medical care.

The use of pesticides is linked to high cancer rates. Toxic symptoms run the gamut from nausea and vomiting to cardiac problems and liver damage. Children are thought to be particularly at risk.

Legal loopholes permit industrial nations to sell banned pesticides to other countries. US Government studies have found that some 25 percent of pesticides sold by the US to foreign countries are banned, restricted, or not even registered. All too often, this creates a "Circle of Poison": the exporting countries may buy fruits, vegetables, and animal products contaminated with the unsafe pesticides which they exported.

Water Pollution—Water, the essential resource which makes life on earth possible, is under siege. As industry and agriculture expand and population grows, water is becoming scarcer and its quality is declining.

In principle, the world water supply should be sufficient to sustain 20 billion people if it is not squandered. But because water sources are unevenly distributed, water is used faster than it is being replaced in some areas. Even now, about 40 percent of the world does not have enough.

Perhaps more immediately dangerous to human health is the deterioration of water quality, assaulted on three fronts—domestic waste water, effluents from industry, and land-use runoff. All three are potential health hazards, especially in developing countries. In poorer nations a scant half of the population has safe drinking water.

Controlling water quality is crucial for the Third World. In addition to other population problems, close to 2.9 billion people have no facilities for sanitary waste disposal. It is hardly surprising that water-borne and water-related diseases claim at least 25 million lives yearly in the poorer regions. In addition to causing high rates of mortality in infants, unclean water is also the source of such water-borne diseases as trachoma, schistosomiasis, cholera, typhoid and many others (*table,* page 38). Polluted water is an increasingly serious problem in rapidly-growing urban centers that suffer from both domestic sewage woes and industrial pollution.

Water-borne diseases are also a growing concern in the developed world. In the US, 15 million people drink from potentially unsafe water supplies. A recent EPA study of municipal water systems in the US revealed that only 60 of the 446 met federal standards. A 1988 study tallied 2,100 contaminants found in US water since the Safe Drinking Water Act was passed in 1974. A number of them were harmful chemicals: 97 were known carcinogens, 82 cause mutations, 28 are toxic, and 23 tumor promoters.

Ozone Layer—Expanding population contributes to less immediate but potentially more dangerous threats to human health. One is the depletion of the stratospheric ozone layer. The other is the "greenhouse effect," which is a harbinger of climate changes thought to be leading inexorably to global warming. Increased industrial activity, the burning of fossil fuels and the use of fertilizers are held responsible for these changes. Chlorofluorocarbons (CFCs), in particular, are known ozone depleters and environmental enemies. They can also cause serious health problems: fatal arrhythmia, lung disease, memory loss, or psychomotor impairment. CFC use in aerosol spray cans was banned in 1978 in the US. Since then, international action has been taken to phase out the compounds by the year 2000 (page 35).

Unlike ground ozone which pollutes the air, stratospheric ozone shields human beings against harmful solar radiation. A significant ozone reduction in the upper atmosphere permits damaging radiation to reach the earth. This could result in dramatic increases in the incidence of cancer and cataracts from UV-B, that part of ultraviolet radiation known to be biologically damaging. The link between UV-B and skin cancer is well known. Even a one percent increase in UV-B because of ozone layer depletion could result in non-melanoma cancers among light skinned people, according to one estimate.

Climate change—As world population grows and the world economy expands, the concentration of heat-trapping gases—most notably CO_2—is increasing. Most scientists agree that this process will bring on drastic climate changes and lead to global warming. Even a warming of 3 degrees Celcius, predicted by the end of the next century, would have dramatic health effects. Medical science estimates that with this extreme warming there would be a rise in deaths due to heat stress, increased incidence of respiratory diseases and of allergic reactions. Older people would suffer more from the effects of heart and respiratory diseases. The mosquito population might increase, and the diseases they transmit multiply. The worst-case scenario would be apocalyptic—scarce food, rising waters, disrupted sanitary facilities and contaminated water supplies, leading to a wave of enteric infections and epidemics.

Even far less dramatic changes in climate, if they come about as predicted, would alter both temperature and rainfall patterns and have a major effect on world food supply, increasing the risk of widespread famine and death. Whatever changes might occur would be irreversible.

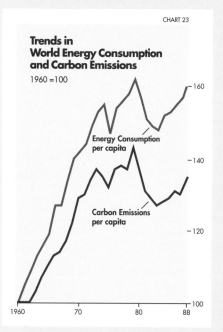

CHART 23

Trends in World Energy Consumption and Carbon Emissions
1960 = 100

Energy Consumption per capita

Carbon Emissions per capita

The renewed rise in energy consumption per capita in the 1980's cancelled earlier economies and once more started dangerous carbon emissions on an upward trend.

Energy—Essential as it is to the modern world, energy exacts a heavy toll in terms of polluted air and water, and darkens the future with the prospect of global warming.

Transportation contributes as much as 90 percent to man-made emissions of carbon dioxide, produced by fossil fuels. Motor vehicles are the prime villains, responsible for threatening levels of CO_2 emissions and CFCs. The gases emitted from vehicle fuel cause a variety of ill effects on health. CO_2 can trigger attacks of angina and cause other serious heart problems. Other pollutants are irritating to the lungs and are responsible for many respiratory complications.

Nuclear energy, linchpin of our atomic age, was once thought to have great potential to supplement the limited resources of fossil fuel. Although clean and virtually inexhaustible, it has become the most controversial of all energy sources, challenged on grounds of health, safety, and environmental damage. Risk is implicit when a sizeable amount of radioactivity is concentrated in one place. The possibility of human failure adds another hazard, since nuclear accidents so far have largely been the result of human error. In the US, 104,000 incidents in which workers were exposed to measurable doses of radiation were recorded in 1987 alone.

The effects of radiation on health are still not completely understood. Critics of nuclear power increasingly feel that even low levels of exposure may be harmful. There is mounting evidence that exposure to low-level radiation in uranium mining, weapons testing, even living in the area of a nuclear facility, may have long term effects on health—birth defects, mental retardation, leukemia and other forms of cancer. Even small amounts of radiation from X rays and other medical procedures are under suspicion.

"We travel together, passengers on a little spaceship, dependent on its vulnerable resources of air and soil; all committed for our safety for its security and peace; preserved from annihilation only by the care, the work, and I will say, the love we give our fragile craft."
Adlai Stevenson, US, 1965

Safeguarding Health

A wide-angle view of the serious health consequences of environmental damage is disquieting and has set off a ground swell of public concern, spurring governments to action. In a recent Harris poll of 16 industrial and developing nations, the public gave a higher priority to reducing the health risks from environmental sources than to improving living standards. Most even expressed a willingness to pay higher taxes to achieve this goal.

Until recently, efforts to protect health have been sporadic and have mainly offered stop-gap remedies. What is needed now is global assessment of environmental health perils and decisive policies to prevent further damage. Together, nations must establish safeguards that will control unbridled population growth, curb pollution of air, land, and water, and limit harmful energy consumption.

Reducing population pressure—Controlling burgeoning population is a critical component of any overall strategy for limiting health damage. Slower population growth would tangibly lessen escalating worldwide demands for energy, reduce the pressure on tillable land, curb the flow of fertilizers and pesticides in water supplies, and protect vital forests and croplands.

Providing pre-natal care which helps both mother and child, improving women's education, and making family planning services available are important safeguards. Spacing births so that they are not less than three years apart and limiting their number is part of a UN goal to achieve an average birth rate of 3.2 children per woman in developing countries by 2000 to 2005. Providing a wide range of methods for spacing births is important; family planning services function best as part of a broader primary health care program and must be adapted to a country's culture.

Population programs should receive a higher proportion of international financial assistance than they do at present. The US contribution to some world population organizations has been substantially cut since 1986.

Improving water quality and supply—As population grows, conserving water and preventing its contamination are increasingly important to protect health, especially in developing countries, but also in the industrial nations.

Improving water collection and storage techniques is a primary safeguard for conserving water resources being drained by industries and crowded urban centers. The world's linked network of rivers, lakes, streams, and oceans demands international cooperation. Efficient management of water resources includes monitoring and judicious decisions in planning dams or canals. Curbing the subsidies of water which mask its true costs would discourage prodigal water use. In the US, where agriculture accounts for 80 percent of national water use, the cost of water is so heavily subsidized in some regions that it is virtually cost-free and used extravagantly.

Important as they are, water development projects—building dams or canals—can damage water quality and ruin farmlands. Controlling these projects that often result in wasteful run-offs, retaining wooded land, and encouraging the re-use of waste water would improve the efficiency of water use. Adopting new micro-irrigation techniques such as the slow-drip method, three times more efficient than traditional methods, would also lessen land runoffs.

Maintaining water quality is an equally challenging goal. The major sources of pollution are organic human waste, synthetic chemicals and heavy metals, and land use runoffs. Human waste is the most serious cause of pollution, especially acute in developing countries.

Controlling sewage disposal is vital. Providing simple low-cost latrines is a cost-effective way of improving sanitary conditions.

Water quality is declining in developed countries as industrial pollutants, pesticides, and other hazardous substances increasingly pervade ground water. Stricter standards should be imposed on waste production and disposal. End-of-pipe remedies for industrial pollution should be replaced by the recycling or re-use of waste water whenever possible. In the US, a slogan of "Pollution Prevention Pays" has spawned some successful industry efforts to recycle waste water and save money as well.

Controlling hazardous substances—The proliferation of hazardous substances and the toxic wastes they produce are endangering not only precious water supplies, but also the air and the soil of the planet. Hazardous substances should be identified and the public informed of the risks involved. The problems of safe disposal of hazardous wastes, including radioactive wastes, are still to be solved satisfactorily. In the US, applying the "Polluter Pays" principle in which the cost of cleanup and disposal is assumed by the polluter, is encouraging cost-effective reductions in waste production. Mounting evidence of the health damage caused by pesticides has not yet slowed their use. As little as 0.1 per cent of the 4 billion pounds sold yearly actually reach the pests which are their targets. Instead, they frequently contaminate the food they are meant to protect.

A number of pesticides too dangerous to be used in the US and other industrialized countries can be sold abroad because of legal loopholes. Adequate regulations and stricter supervision would safeguard the health of both exporting countries and those which import the pesticides and frequently do not take proper precautions in using them. Imported food should be inspected for traces of banned pesticides, and limits set for the amounts permitted to remain on them. The US Congress is considering legislation to bar the export of pesticides, and not surprisingly, encountering resistance from the chemical industry.

Safer ways of controlling pests should be adopted more widely. Integrated Pest Management (IPM), a combination of biological controls, natural products, and planting practices such as: crop rotation, which discourages a large number of pests; intercropping (glossary p. 61); and seeding areas with natural predators that feed on pests are proving successful. In El Salvador, seeding an area with a wasp that eats the eggs of some agricultural pests eliminated the need for 10 pesticide applications each season.

Reducing Air Pollution—The noxious substances spewed into the air by ever-growing numbers of motor vehicles and by the burning of fossil fuels are grave current perils; in addition they are contributing to future climate warming. Clearing the air requires a major decrease in all pollutants.

Safeguarding the earth's ozone layer demands the virtual elimination of all stratospheric ozone-depleting CFCs. A mandatory, gradual phase-out has already begun as a result of the 1990 amended version of the Montreal Protocol (page 35). For the first time, financial help to developing countries to enable them to make the technological transition is included in the agreement.

In the US large companies are already using new techniques to bypass CFC use. In the meantime, governments can help by setting stringent health and safety standards, limiting ambient CFC levels around factories, and imposing penalties for careless release. Also essential is the restoration of some of the lost forest cover which has permitted the release of massive quantities of carbon dioxide, methane, and other gases.

Improving energy efficiency—Reducing fossil fuel use and its carbon dioxide emissions, the chief source of greenhouse gases and so costly to human health, demands a profound restructuring of energy policies. Great strides have been made in developing non-polluting renewable forms of energy such as solar and wind power, but prospects for their replacing fossil fuels are, at the moment, still remote. Increasing R&D efforts to improve renewable energy potential however, should be a major international goal.

Another, and more immediate, target is to improve energy efficiency (see page 34). Maintaining current levels of activity on a reduced amount of energy will slow the progression of acid rain, smog, and other threats to health. It will also deter the building of new power plants. Since transportation, especially motor vehicles, represent the largest drain on world oil reserves, car pooling, walking, bicycling, or using public transportation should replace car use whenever possible. Driving fuel-efficient vehicles that get at least 30 to 35 mpg also cuts down gasoline consumption substantially.

Taxation is a painful but highly effective way to achieve energy conservation. A carbon tax on the use of fossil fuels has been useful. Finland introduced the first carbon tax in 1990; Sweden soon followed. A meaningful gasoline tax would save fuel and generate substantial revenues that could be spent to improve mass transportation. The US median gasoline tax is still far lower than in Europe, about one eighth of the average (*chart 24*).

Regulation is also an essential tool. The average new American car is well below the average new car in fuel economy. Environmentalists estimate that by increasing US fuel economy standards to 40 mpg, a feasible objective for the years ahead (*chart 25*), the US could save 8 to 9 billion barrels of oil by 2010. Computer-controlled timing of traffic signals that improve traffic flow helps cut down CO_2 emissions; 25 gallons of fuel are saved for every dollar spent.

Cost-benefits—Even when cost estimates for preventing pollution or the depletion of natural resources seem expensive, the cost of repairing damage after it occurs is much greater, especially in terms of human health. For example, in Canada it is estimated that reducing carbon emissions by 20 percent would cost the government $108 billion but ultimately save $190 billion in averted health damage. For more efficient lighting, compact fluorescent lamps and sensors that turn lights off in unoccupied rooms are all energy savers. One compact fluorescent bulb delivers as much light as an incandescent bulb, which consumes four times as much electricity. Insulating homes fully by caulking, weather-stripping windows, or using storm windows, all help to keep heat in and energy bills down. In India a single million dollar factory could produce enough fluorescent light bulbs to save the country $204 billion annually, mainly from not having to build additional power plants.

Low-cost, even no-cost, measures demonstrably conserve energy or water. Low-flush toilets need less than one-fourth the standard amount of water. Low-flush shower heads also conserve a considerable amount of water, as do car-wash facilities that use recycled water. Reducing garbage and recycling wastes are energy-efficient as well. In the US, enough wood and paper is thrown away each year to heat five million homes for 200 years.

The sun's energy can be utilized in simple, efficient ways. Especially in developing countries that can depend on numerous hours of sunlight a season, the sun's energy can be used to purify lightly polluted water; two to five hours of sunlight render almost 100 percent of the bacteria harmless, lessening the need for fuelwood to boil water. Waste water lagoons exposed to the sun and using certain types of algae have been found to produce relatively potable water after a number of days; in Chile, water heated with this process for 20 days had less bacteria than nearby tap water. Simple, low-cost solar cookers also reduce the need for firewood. For every dollar spent on biological crop controls on the cassava harvest in 19 African countries, $140 is returned in improved yield of cassavas, a principal source of protein for millions of rural Africans.

Whether cost-effective or not, efforts to conserve human resources will ultimately benefit human health. Even when the price tags of health-protecting measures seem disproportionate, they are often outweighed by the benefits they bestow. In time, a collective international effort to reorder priorities may restore the primeval and prized balance between people and their habitat.

CHART 24

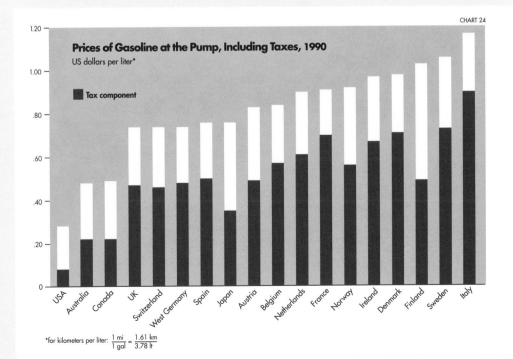

Prices of Gasoline at the Pump, Including Taxes, 1990
US dollars per liter*

■ Tax component

USA, Australia, Canada, UK, Switzerland, West Germany, Spain, Japan, Austria, Belgium, Netherlands, France, Norway, Ireland, Denmark, Finland, Sweden, Italy

*for kilometers per liter: $\frac{1 \text{ mi}}{1 \text{ gal}} = \frac{1.61 \text{ km}}{3.78 \text{ lt}}$

CHART 25

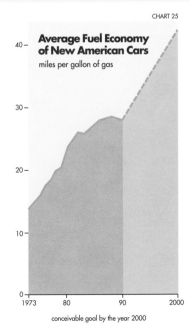

Average Fuel Economy of New American Cars
miles per gallon of gas

1973 80 90 2000

conceivable goal by the year 2000

Changing Direction

Triumphs in technology and the growth of the world economy have created in us a sense of progress and security. Yet an unflinching look at the state of the world today proves this perception to be mere illusion. We are not yet masters of the universe; in fact, our world seems to be spinning out of control toward an uncertain conclusion. Population is exploding, poverty rampant, resources shrinking. Global atmospheric changes threaten our health today and the survival of the human race in the future.

We have also been slow to react to these dangers with the energy and creativity of which we are capable. A collective effort of will must be summoned to overcome world inertia. To change direction, to act responsibly, new priorities must be set, and hard fiscal decisions taken. A global fund of **$45 billion annually** for protection of our environment could make a difference worldwide in how well we live and how long.

The bill for environmental action may seem high at first. But improving the quality of the air can be a surprising bargain in terms of lives saved, structural damage averted, and health care expenses avoided. Investing in renewable energy can result in greater economic security. And surely holding off the onset of possible global warming and climate change, with its virtually unlimited potential for harm, is a responsibility we cannot afford to shirk.

Whatever sums must be allocated today for the sake of tomorrow are dwarfed by the trillions of dollars that have been squandered on massive military preparations. Consider what could be done for the public's health and the survival of the planet with a small fraction (5 percent) of the $900 billion now devoted yearly to weapons and warfare:

Reforest the earth .... **$2 billion**

The tropical forests are disappearing at the rate of 13 to 20 million hectares per year. Forest destruction leads to rapid loss of soil and of nutrient sources, affecting the lives of one-fifth of humanity. It also contributes to global warming. A worldwide citizen program should plant several billion trees yearly.

or buy another nuclear-armed submarine.

Provide safe water .... **$5 billion**

One-third of the world population lacks an accessible supply of safe water. Impure water is a contributing cause of 80 percent of Third World diseases, including cholera. Developing countries should be provided with stand pipes, hand pumps, water taps, or other basic means of access to safe water.

or make more nuclear bombs.

Roll back the desert .... **$2 billion**

Over six million hectares—one-third of the world's cropland—are turning into dessert, shrinking the growing area that is vital for food supplies. Multiplying populations denude fertile lands by overuse. Proper soil and water management, with protective planting, could restore arable land.

or conduct a dozen nuclear weapon tests.

Protect the ozone layer .... **$1 billion**

A total ban of CFCs and other chemicals which deplete the protective ozone layer is an urgent global priority. Finding substitutes for CFCs and converting current technology is beyond the means of many Third World nations. Helping them financially to make the transition will speed ozone layer protection.

or send the space shuttle on more flights for Star Wars.

Reduce air pollution .... **$5 billion**

Pollutants in the air threaten world health. They are causing an increasing number of acute and chronic illnesses. In the US alone some 150 million people live in areas with air unfit to breathe. Reducing emissions of 191 toxic chemicals should be a worldwide goal.

or invest in six more Stealth nuclear bombers.

Conserve natural assets .... **$4 billion**

Many Third World countries try to maintain their land for agriculture and their forests for living species and for fuel, but lack both the knowledge and the resources to solve the complex problems they face. Providing them with expert guidance and sufficient funds would help them preserve vital natural assets.

or send some arms to the Middle East.

Stabilize population .... **$6 billion**

Rapid population growth is regarded by many as the single greatest threat to the planet's health. Yet in developing countries family planning services are not available for 100 million couples who want them. Family planning along with universal female literacy are essentials for population stabilization.

or send more arms to the Middle East.

Clean up hazardous wastes .... **$10 billion**

A lethal mix of toxic wastes, including radioactive elements, contaminates the soil and water in hundreds of thousands of sites worldwide. Finding safe ways to clean up toxins and store wastes is essential. Cleanup costs, though high, are only a fraction of the costs in terms of human lives and human health.

or send still more arms to the Middle East.

Increase research to protect the environment .... **$10 billion**

There are many alternatives to the fossil fuels which pollute the atmosphere, damage forests and lakes, and create the greenhouse effect which is in turn destroying the earth's protective ozone layer. Renewable, living, sources of energy include solar energy, tidal energy, geothermal, hydropower, biomass. Their commercial possibilities have not been vigorously pursued, nor publicly subsidized as nuclear power has been.

There are also many energy conservation efforts which are not yet adequately exploited. Publicly-financed research programs have given them short shrift. The contrast with the R&D invested in weapons is especially pronounced. Industrial countries spend about $110 billion a year on government R&D, of which 47 percent has gone to the military, 4 percent to energy, 1 percent to control of environmental pollution. What a difference a wealth of R&D can make: new American cars are twice as fuel-efficient as they were 20 years ago, but American weapons are 100 times as efficient—in accuracy and destructiveness. The opportunities for environmental gains clearly are wide open.

Or put a down-payment on NASA's $120 billion space station.

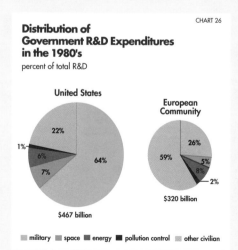

Distribution of Government R&D Expenditures in the 1980's

percent of total R&D

CHART 26

United States

22%
1%
6%
7%
64%
$467 billion

European Community

26%
5%
8%
2%
59%
$320 billion

■ military ■ space ■ energy ■ pollution control ■ other civilian

Opportunities

The neglected environment speaks eloquently to the tragic distortion of the world's priorities. An obsession with military power as a quick fix for political problems has left us with a gross oversupply of weapons and a dangerous backlog of unmet needs for which military superiority is not merely irrelevant but counterproductive.

The problems of today are too complex for military resolution. The big issues, whether political, economic-social, or environmental, transcend national boundaries—as do the solutions. For these reasons, the need to move away from our military preoccupations goes beyond the financial aspects. Real-world priorities call for dedicated international collaboration, a spirit incompatible with a consuming arms race and the rivalry and tensions that it fosters. If countries can form a victorious coalition to oust an aggressor, as they did in 1990–91, surely they can work together more effectively than they have in the past on the big problems they have in common.

How to break the log-jam? First, of course, is to recognize that sustained militarism has major responsibility for it and that spending priorities must change. Out of a global military budget which still exceeds $900 billion in current values, enormous savings are possible. While official negotiations in early 1991 appear to have lost momentum, the international climate is basically favorable and presents unparalleled opportunities, both through negotiations and supporting actions, to achieve big reductions in world military expenditures. This is a juncture in time when active public support is critical.

Formal disarmament negotiations

If a wish list were based on actions not yet taken to control/reduce military forces and expenditures, the possibilities for international agreements would seem boundless. For example, despite the more than three decades of disarmament negotiations since World War II:

- **Of the major weapons of mass destruction, nuclear, chemical, and biological, only the last has been banned. There is no overall prohibition as yet on the development or possession of nuclear or chemical weapons.**

- **Nor is there a comprehensive ban on the testing of nuclear weapons or missiles.**

- **While nuclear and missile proliferation in the Third World is now the subject of increasing concern, the superpowers in their negotiations have been slow to reduce their own huge inventories, and the other nuclear powers have not started such negotiations.**

- **The recent landmark treaty on conventional forces in Europe (CFE), while shrinking the big Warsaw Pact advantage in the number of major weapons, does not appreciably reduce NATO's weapons below present holdings, nor does it restrict naval forces, men under arms, or investment in new conventional weapons.**

- **The trade in conventional arms is not limited by treaty.**

- **No treaty provides for a "peace dividend," a reduction in military expenditures commensurate with the reduction of forces.**

An additional feature missing from virtually all the negotiations on disarmament is speed. Efforts for a nuclear test ban went on for 8 years until the compromise, or limited, test ban treaty of 1963; even START, the strategic arms reduction treaty, has taken 9 years, although there have been negotiations on strategic arms since 1969. If past history is a guide, formal negotiations are unlikely to come to fruition rapidly or to produce big money savings for the 1990's.

Nevertheless, with Europe's rebirth and the end of the cold war, there is no question that major cutbacks in weapons, forces, and fleets should be pursued through international negotiations. This is the only approach which can ensure satisfactory verification, and lock in whatever gains are made. Progress in this form also improves the general climate for de-militarization and for restrictions on military budgets. A few of the possibilities are outlined below.

"Without disarmament there can be no lasting peace. On the contrary, the continuation of military armaments in their present extent will with certainty lead to new catastrophes."

Albert Einstein
Germany, 1931

Arms Control and Disarmament Agreements*

The stately pace of official disarmament negotiations during 1990 contrasted with the extraordinary and rapid political changes underway in Europe. Though disappointingly slow, there was some progress in three areas:

The star achievement was an agreement on a significant reduction of NATO and Warsaw Pact conventional forces in Europe, completed and signed by the 22 member nations after only 20 months of negotiations. The CFE Treaty has not yet been ratified.

A treaty for the reduction of nuclear weapons, an effort which has been underway in various forums since 1969, was essentially completed but signing of START was delayed for a US-USSR Summit meeting, now scheduled for a date before mid-1991.

The US and USSR agreed to reduce their enormous stocks of chemical weapons. Meanwhile negotiations for a multilateral convention banning development, production, and stockpiling of chemical weapons continued for the 10th year.

Nuclear Weapons

To prevent the spread of nuclear weapons—
Antarctic Treaty, 1959   **39 states[1]**
Bans any military uses of Antarctica and specifically prohibits nuclear tests and nuclear waste.

Outer Space Treaty, 1967   **90 states[1]**
Bans nuclear weapons in earth orbit and their stationing in outer space.

Latin American Nuclear-Free Zone Treaty, 1967   **23 states[1]**
Bans testing, possession, deployment of nuclear weapons and requires safeguards on facilities.

Non-Proliferation Treaty, 1968   **141 states[1]**
Bans transfer of weapons or weapons technology to non-nuclear weapons states. Requires safeguards on their facilities. Commits nuclear-weapon states to negotiations to halt the arms race.

Seabed Treaty, 1971   **80 states[1]**
Bans nuclear weapons on the seabed beyond a 12-mile coastal limit.

South Pacific Nuclear-Free Zone Treaty, 1985   **11 states[1]**
Bans testing, manufacture, acquisition, stationing of nuclear weapons. Requests five nuclear weapons states to sign a protocol banning use or threat of nuclear weapons and nuclear testing.[4]

To limit nuclear testing—
Limited Nuclear Test Ban Treaty, 1963   **116 states[1]**
Bans nuclear weapons tests in the atmosphere, outer space, or underwater. Bans underground explosions which cause release of radioactive debris beyond the state's borders.

Threshold Test Ban Treaty, 1974   **US—USSR**
Bans underground tests having a yield above 150 kilotons (150,000 tons of TNT equivalent).

Peaceful Nuclear Explosions Treaty, 1976   **US—USSR**
Bans "group explosion" with aggregate yield over 1,500 kilotons and requires on-site observers of group explosions over 150 kilotons.

To reduce the risk of nuclear war—
Hot Line and Modernization Agreements, 1963   US—USSR
Establishes direct radio and wire-telegraph links between Moscow and Washington to ensure communication in times of crisis. 1971 agreement provided for satellite communication circuits.

Accidents Measures Agreement, 1971   **US—USSR**
Pledges US and USSR to improve safeguards against accidental or unauthorized use of nuclear weapons.

Prevention of Nuclear War Agreement, 1973   **US—USSR**
Requires consultation between the two countries if their is a danger of nuclear war.

Nuclear Risk Reduction Centers, 1987   **US—USSR**
Establishes high speed communication centers in Washington and Moscow.

To limit nuclear weapons—
ABM Treaty (SALT I) and Protocol, 1972, 1974   US—USSR
Limits anti-ballistic missile systems to one deployment area on each side. Bans nationwide anti-ballistic missile system, and development testing, or deployment of sea-based, air-based, or space-based ABM system.

SALT I Interim Agreement, 1972   **US—USSR**
Freezes the number of strategic ballistic missile launchers, and permits an increase in SLBM launchers up to an agreed level only with equivalent dismantling of older ICBM or SLBM launchers.

SALT II, 1979   **US—USSR[3]**
Limits numbers of strategic nuclear delivery vehicles, launchers of MIRV'd missiles, bombers with long-range cruise missiles, warheads on existing ICBM's, etc. Bans testing or deploying new ICBM's.

INF Treaty, 1987   **US—USSR**
Eliminates US and USSR ground-level intermediate- and shorter-range missiles (ranges of 300 to 3,500 miles). Requires dismantling within 3 years; extensive verification provisions.

Other Weapons

To prohibit use of gas—
Geneva Protocol, 1925   **123 states[1]**
Bans the use in war of asphyxiating, poisonous, or other gases, and of bacteriological methods of warfare.

To prohibit biological weapons—
Biological Weapons Convention, 1972   **110 states[1]**
Bans the development, production, and stockpiling of biological and toxin weapons; requires the destruction of stocks.

To prohibit techniques changing the environment—
Environmental Modification Convention, 1977   **52 states[1]**
Bans military or other hostile use of techniques to change weather or climate patterns, ocean currents, ozone layer, or ecological balance.

To control use of inhumane weapons—
Inhumane Weapons Convention, 1981   **30 states[1]**
Bans use of fragmentation bombs not detectable in the human body; bans use against civilians of mines, booby traps, and incendiary weapons; requires record-keeping on mines.

To limit conventional forces—
Conventional Forces in Europe, 1990   **22 states[2]**
Puts explicit limits on five major categories of military equipment in Europe, for a NATO-WP balance of forces at lower levels.

To destroy chemical agents—
Chemical Agreement, 1990   **US—USSR[2]**
Obliges US and USSR to destroy stocks of chemical weapons to maximum of 5,000 tons by the year 2002.

Dates shown are dates agreements were signed. 1. Number of ratifications as recorded (by Westing Associates, Putney, VT, USA) from the records of the depositaries, as of March 1991.   2. Not ratified.   3. Not ratified but observed in 5-year duration of the treaty.

Negotiation forums now in existence provide numerous opportunities for action. Ideally, the next round on conventional weapons (CFE IA) would include: deeper cuts in weapons stationed in Europe and their destruction rather than re-deployment or sale; the reduction of armed forces (beyond national plans already in effect); and restraints on weapons modernization. A limit on the procurement of major conventional weapons would put a needed cap on quality upgrading and would also be a great money saver. In early 1991 it seems unlikely that the current forum will get that far this year, but more is expected of follow-on negotiations in 1992, which will also involve 34 nations, 12 more than in the present CFE.

For the control of nuclear weapons the basic requirement, in the view of most specialists, is agreement on a Comprehensive Test Ban (CTB). This will require strong public pressure in the US and UK, the only countries which were determined holdouts at the Limited Test Ban review meeting in January 1991. A complete ban on nuclear tests is essential to prevent continuing modernization, and to reenforce the nonproliferation regime. Further support for the two objectives would come from a halt in production of both new nuclear weapons and the fissile materials (plutonium and highly enriched uranium) for weapons. Now that the first significant cuts have been made in stocks, START must strive for much bigger reductions in strategic nuclear weapons (e.g., a 50 percent cutback in the next session) and move more decisively to control quality enhancement, which will be the main focus of the arms race in nuclear as well as conventional weapons.

Supplementary actions

If there is political will—which usually means strong public pressure—there are also many opportunities for moves outside of treaty negotiations to achieve arms control and even disarmament. Restrictions on chemical weapons are illustrative. It looks now as though an international treaty banning these weapons is near—according to some optimists, possibly this year or next. At the same time, there are efforts underway to tighten export controls on chemicals through an informal suppliers group of 20 industrial countries, the Australia Group, which meets twice yearly for this purpose.

Unilateral actions to curb the spread of chemicals and other weapons of mass destruction are also being taken. The US recently announced new export controls including: a five-fold increase in the number of chemicals requiring license for export and, for the first time, controls on equipment to make the weapons. The restrictions are to apply to all 14 Middle East countries, including US allies.

The 15-nation Missile Technology Control Regime (MTCR) is another existing suppliers group. MTCR is now discussing tighter and tougher controls on exports of technology which can be used to manufacture long-range missiles. The Federation of American Scientists (FAS), in a 5-point plan for the Middle East (see brief outline above), has suggested a broadening of the group both in membership and coverage. The FAS plan is interesting in another respect: it includes the use of economic measures to enforce the arms restraints.

Economic leverage to promote arms control and reduction has considerable potential, but has too seldom been applied for this purpose. Its utility has been dramatically demonstrated in

---

Spotlight on the Middle East

A 5-point plan for arms control by the Federation of American Scientists.

1. **Restrict trade in missiles**—Press all states capable of producing missiles to join the Missile Technology Control Regime (MTCR) and pledge to follow its restraints on sales of ballistic missiles or components.
2. **Control trade in other weapons**—US should discuss with USSR and West European suppliers the extension of MTCR model to other major equipment, including tanks and attack aircrafts.
3. **Enforce restraints**—Use both economic (e.g. blacklisting) and diplomatic pressure against companies and countries violating controls.
4. **Start confidence-building measures**—To improve the climate for disarmament, urge Middle East to make no-first-use pledge on missiles, and take other reassuring steps.
5. **Try for arms moratorium**—Initiate agreement for 5-year moratorium on arms sales to the region by five permanent members of Security Council (US, USSR, UK, France, China).

---

the Gulf War, where it was used as both carrot and stick. The trade embargo against Iraq proved to be highly effective and durable and, at the end of the conflict, the principal means of enforcing the terms of the peace. On the positive side, debt relief and other prizes were used to draw countries into the coalition against Iraq (e.g., for Egypt, debt forgiveness of $7 billion by the US alone) and to strengthen the embargo by compensating poorer countries for loss of exports and tourism (e.g., for Turkey, supplementary aid and trade concessions).

There is no reason why economic clout would not be equally effective in direct support of arms restraint. In apportioning its aid among developing countries, Japan is taking their military expenditures into account. Other donors and international agencies could adopt this pressure more broadly. In the same way, economic inducements can be used to foster arms control. China, for one, might be persuaded to forego proliferation of missiles and other destabilizing weapons if there were some compensation for lost export sales.

Another economic-disarmament connection is critically important, and that is a more binding tie between disarmament and budgetary savings than we have had in the past. The tradition in negotiations is to emphasize political-military objectives; a prime consideration is negotiating for military advantage. After decades of support for disarmament negotiations, however, taxpayers are owed some compensation in the form of a lower military burden. What they have seen so far—after 30 years of formal talks—is more than a doubling of world military expenditures in real terms. They might begin to get more visible benefits if official instructions to negotiators also included objectives in terms of budgetary savings and if national executives were obliged to make a yearly public report on progress in reducing arms *and* military budgets.

This link would help to get the new world order off to a running start. It might also have the effect of taking disarmament negotiations out of the dark, mysterious closet in which they generally reside. Besides clear financial benefits, the public needs more information about what is going on. The radio-TV programs are displayed in the newspapers daily, the latest scores of the ball games at least weekly. Where does one go for a regular update on the biggest game of all, the game of international security? At stake is the $900 billion that comes out of taxpayers' pockets every year. ☐

CHART 27

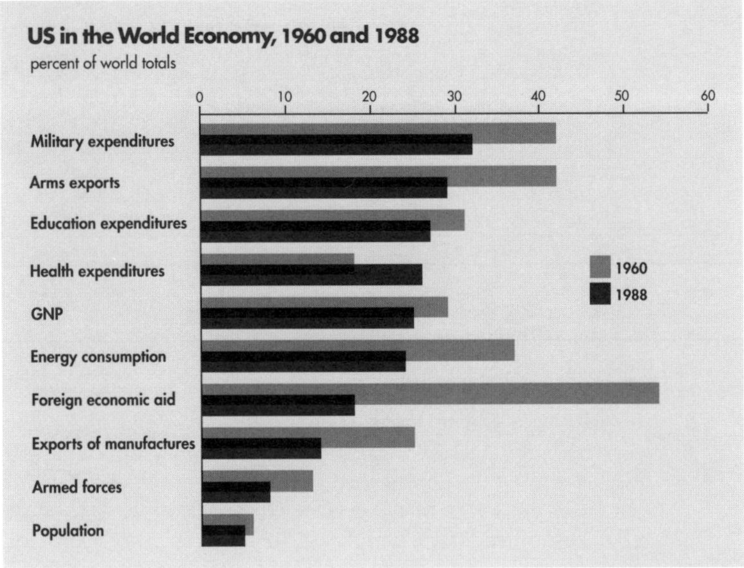
US in the World Economy, 1960 and 1988
percent of world totals
0
10
20
30
40
50
60
Military expenditures
Arms exports
Education expenditures
Health expenditures
GNP
Energy consumption
Foreign economic aid
Exports of manufactures
Armed forces
Population
1960
1988

The Superpower

With two successful and brief wars in a span of less than fourteen months*, the US remains a military superpower—no longer as Number One, now essentially the Only One. The decline in the Soviet military presence and prestige, along with the quiet revolution in Eastern Europe in 1989, has changed the nature of the competition in much of the world. In 1990 the two powers broke with their past pattern of mutual hostility to establish close communications and even to collaborate in peace missions in the developing world. Independently the US also took an increasingly active role as world policeman. In August 1990 it singlehandedly assumed reponsibility for the management of a major multi-national intervention in the Middle East and in January 1991 led allied forces in a quick, victorious war against the aggressor.

The Gulf War was a clear win for US military technology and put it solidly in first place, ready for whatever the nature of the future arms race will be. The Pentagon plans to keep it that way and has designed a large menu of advanced weapons. While the military budget is being squeezed down (a modest 3 percent a year), the spotlight in the budget plan for FY 1992 continues to be on new weapons technology. Compared with the beginning of the buildup in 1980, defense R & D will be up 79 percent in real terms.

The US competitive position in civilian markets is not nearly as solid as it is in military goods, and it is hardly likely that even a big push in arms exports (as suggested by the Administration) could make a major difference in the American share of total trade. The US accounts for about one-third of global arms exports but the arms trade represent a very small fraction (about 2 percent) of world trade. As *chart 27* indicates, the US now has a 15 percent share of world exports of manufactured goods. Gone are the days when it commanded a share more in line with its dominant position in global GNP.

The table opposite, on US rank among the countries covered in this study, illustrates the sharp dichotomy between two major elements of America's international standing. In military power, US eminence is clear. In social development, it lags, sometimes falling behind the average for other industrial countries despite its rank in per capita GNP. Public expenditures and the indicators shown on *chart 27,* also underline these contrasts. Whether measured in budgets, trade, or the relative increase in armed forces compared with population. US priorities emphasize military over social objectives.

Historical change

The historical record (*chart 28*) indicates that the US status as a military superstar began only after World War II. Before that war there were at least eight major military states: based on League of Nations records, the line-up then also put US in first place, but only marginally ahead of France, UK, and USSR. Below, in second rank, were Italy, Japan, Germany, and Poland. In the period before the war, the US accounted for about 15 percent of world military expenditures. Its military budget hovered around 1 percent of its GNP.

US Rank Among 142 Countries

Military Power	
Military expenditures	1
Military technology	1
Military bases world-wide	1
Military training of foreign forces	1
Military aid to foreign countries	1
Naval fleet	1
Combat aircraft	1
Nuclear reactors	1
Nuclear warheads and bombs	1
Nuclear tests	1
Arms exports	2
Armed forces	3
Social Development	
Percent population with safe water	1
Percent school-age children in school	1
Female literacy rate	4
Male literacy rate	4
Per capita public expenditure for education	8
GNP per capita	8
Maternal mortality rate	13
Per capita public expenditure for health	14
Life expectancy (years)	15
Infant mortality rate	18
Population per physician	18
Total fertility rate	20
Percent population with access to sanitation	20
Under 5 mortality rate	22
Percent infants with low birthweight	36

*The US invasion of Panama was on December 20, 1989; the intervention against Iraq on August 2, 1990; and the formal start of the Gulf War on January 16, 1991.

US Public Expenditures, Military, Education, Health

CHART 28

billion 1980 dollars

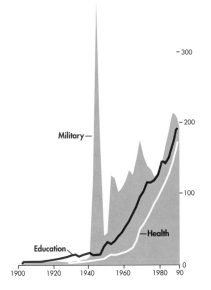

At the end of World War II, US military expenditures did not return to pre-war levels. The Korean War in 1950 was reason for a renewed buildup, raising US budgets sharply to levels from which they never really retreated. The cold war was on, and in a sense the US had already staked out for itself the role of world policeman.

From about $7–9 billion just before World War II, US military budgets in the 1950's escalated to a peacetime minimum of $100 billion a year (all comparisons in 1980 prices). By 1985 they were twice that level, and more than 6 percent of the GNP. Despite Gorbachev's revolutionary changes in the USSR and Eastern Europe, which in practical terms radically altered the US-USSR relationship and ended the cold war, US military expenditures have continued to cling close to the post-World War II peak. As an economic power, the US remains the world's largest by far, with 25 percent of the global GNP. But in its military role it has taken a position beyond its economic strength, draining its economy with a military budget close to one-third of the world's total military expenditures.

A Drag on the Economy

The impact of this strong commitment to military power is felt throughout the US economy, and the consequences, as the examples given below suggest, have not been favorable for US growth or its competitiveness in international markets.

The deficit soars—Unprecedented expenditures for national defense in the 1980's left behind a legacy of unprecedented deficits in the Federal Government's budget. The increase in the annual defense budget from fiscal year 1980 to 1991 amounted to $164 billion, or even more than the $146 billion increase in the overall deficit (*chart 29*). Large government deficits tend to act as a drag on the economy. They reduce resources available for savings, which may in turn have the effect of curtailing investment in growth-producing physical and human capital.

Per capita growth lags—The US economy is now in a downswing, which is expected to be of short duration, but over a longer span of years there are signs that the economy has lost some of its upward momentum. On a per capita basis, economic growth has diminished. In the 1960's, per capita GDP grew at an average annual rate of 3.2 percent; in the 1970's and 1980's, the growth rate has averaged under 2 percent.

Productivity suffers—In manufacturing productivity (output per hour), the US growth rate has been declining since the early 1970's. As shown on *chart 14*, page 27, the US had the lowest annual gain in productivity from 1960 to 1988 of the nine "western" industrial countries. (The USSR, according to CIA, was even more of a laggard in productivity.) Data for 1989, which are now available, show no improvement in the US comparative standing. Its 2 percent increase in productivity from 1988 to 1989 was surpassed by all but one of the industrial countries included in the sample.

Civilian research is neglected—In official US research programs, military defense and space have received 71 percent of total government funds, while in the European Community their share has been only 31 percent. As a result, research related to the competitive international market has had less public funding in the US than in the European Community. During the 1980's, US outlays for civilian-type research were about $9 billion less per year.

Social impact

If the superpower burden has seemed to weigh heavily on the US economy, it has also had a chilling effect on the priority given to social development. The fiscal squeeze has sharply limited services for the poor, affecting such programs as food aid for families with dependent children, nutrition for the elderly, subsidized housing, education loans, and job training. A country which creates the largest annual income in the world has an appalling range of social problems waiting for attention. A quick look at three on which there is mounting pressure for action indicates that there are legitimate reasons for concern.

CHART 29

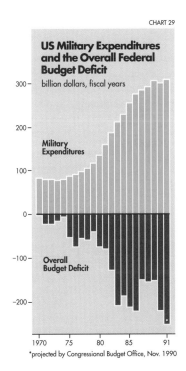

US Military Expenditures and the Overall Federal Budget Deficit

billion dollars, fiscal years

Military Expenditures

Overall Budget Deficit

*projected by Congressional Budget Office, Nov. 1990

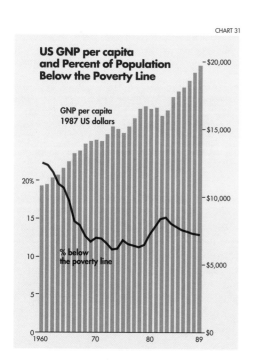

CHART 30

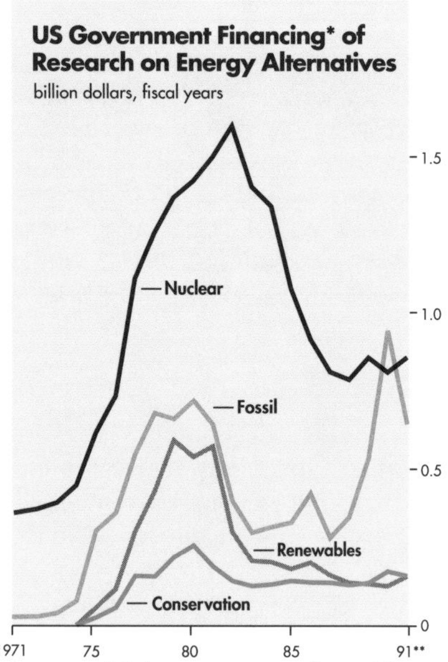

US Government Financing* of Research on Energy Alternatives

billion dollars, fiscal years

— Nuclear

— Fossil

— Renewables

— Conservation

1971   75   80   85   91**

*Series not completely homogeneous: represents obligations before 1978, budget authority beginning 1978.

**1991 proposed

In publicly-funded research on energy alternatives, the US has given priority to energy sources which are not environment-friendly . . . Since 1971, $19 billion have gone to nuclear power research, $8 billion to fossil fuels; in contrast, only $4 billion have been spent on renewable energy sources, $2 billion on conservation.

CHART 31

US GNP per capita and Percent of Population Below the Poverty Line

GNP per capita 1987 US dollars

% below the poverty line

1960   70   80   89

Education—The US is one of the very few developed countries spending less public funds on education than on defense; the only others are USSR, Israel, and former East Germany. In per capita education expenditures, the US ranks 8th among all countries. It does less well in terms of attainment.

• In tests of 12th graders in 12 industrial countries, American students ranked 9th in physics, 11th in chemistry and math, and 12th in biology.
• In a geography test given to 18- to 24-year-olds in 9 countries, Americans in that age group came in last.
• A Federal survey in 1990 found that only 12 percent of American 17-year-olds could read well enough to understand a 12th-grade history textbook.

Health—Public spending on health increased from 1.3 to 4.6 percent of GNP between 1960 and 1987; on a per capita basis it jumped from $133 to $852, more than a six-fold increase in constant prices. At this spending level, US outlays per capita exceed the developed countries' average by 30 percent.

The anomaly in this record is that the US, alone of the developed countries has no public system providing health care protection for all or most of the population. As a result, an estimated 31 to 37 million people in the US do not have any health insurance, public or private.

When private spending is added to public, the US annual health bill is double the average for the industrial countries. The performance record, however, is far from satisfactory:

• In infant mortality, the US stands 18th in rank among all countries; in under-5 mortality, it is 22nd; in infants with low birthweight, 36th.
• Preventable infections, such as measles and whooping cough, once nearly eradicated in the US, are on the rise again apparently due to a low budget and an indifferent record on immunizations.
• Average life expectancy of 75 years puts the US rank at 15 among all countries; the gap between whites and blacks has widened to 6.4 years.

Poverty—The growth of the US economy since 1960 is measured in a remarkable 82 percent rise in real GNP per capita. This progress, however, has not been reflected in a better life for more people. Trends show a widening disparity in US incomes and since the 1970's a greater number of people living in poverty.

During the 1960's, as the average GNP per capita rose, there was a clear drop in the proportion of the population officially classified as poor (*chart 31*). This relationship did not continue after 1969. In 1989, the latest year for which official data are available, 12.8 percent of the US population lived below the poverty level, about the same proportion as at the beginning of the 1970's, although the numbers were higher.

The rising numbers of the poor in a period of sharp economic gains reflect a growing gap in income between rich and poor in the US—a gap which may now be larger than in any other advanced industrial socity. Families in the richest fifth of the US population now have 44.6 percent of all income, the highest share on record. The poorest have 4.6 percent, the lowest on record.

Poverty in America has many faces. It means hungry children, low birthweight babies, single-parent families, homelessness, a more chaotic family life, drugs, violence. The numbers are grim:

• 32 million people live below the official poverty line.
• One child in five is poor, twice the child-poverty rate in Canada, Sweden, and Germany.
• Nearly one-quarter of poor families live in housing officially classified as inadequate.
• 5.5 million children under 12 suffer from hunger.

Poverty is a picture of deteriorating security within a country overly armed for battle abroad.   □

The principal data sources* used in Tables I–III and throughout the book are listed first under each topic. Organizations referred to in the text or notes are shown with their initials.

Population
United Nations (UN), US Bureau of the Census, Population Reference Bureau, Food and Agriculture Organization of the United Nations (FAO).

Education
UNESCO, International Monetary Fund (IMF), United Nations (UN), US Agency for International Development, Organization for Economic Cooperation and Development (OECD), US Bureau of the Census, World Bank, US National Center for Education Statistics.

Environment
World Resources Institute, UN Environmental Programme, UN Statistical Office, Organization for Economic Cooperation and Development, US Energy Information Administration.

Exchange Rates
International Monetary Fund (IMF), Joint Economic Committee of US Congress, World Bank.

Food
Food and Agriculture Organization of the United Nations (FAO), US Department of Agriculture, Brown University (The Hunger Project).

Foreign Aid and Trade
Organization for Economic Cooperation and Development (OECD), US Central Intelligence Agency (CIA), UN Conference on Trade and Development.

Gross National Product
World Bank, Joint Economic Committee of the US Congress, US Department of State, Central Intelligence Agency (CIA), Organization for Economic Cooperation and Development (OECD).

Health
World Health Organization (WHO), Pan American Health Organization (PAHO), Organization for Economic Cooperation and Development (OECD), International Monetary Fund (IMF), US Department of Health and Human Services, US Bureau of the Census, Population Reference Bureau, CREDOC Division d'Economie Medicale, International Social Security Association, Urban Institute, UN Children's Fund (UNICEF), UN Population Fund, UN Population Division, UN Development Programme, Inter-American Development Bank, *Europa Yearbook.*

Military
International Institute for Strategic Studies (IISS), United Nations (UN), North Atlantic Treaty Organization (NATO), Stockholm International Peace Research Institute (SIPRI), International Monetary Fund (IMF), Joint Economic Committee of the US Congress, *The Stateman's Yearbook, Arms Control Today,* US Arms Control and Disarmament Agency (ACDA), US Central Intelligence Agency (CIA), US Defense Intelligence Agency (DIA), Center for Defense Information, Comptroller General of the US, US Department of Defense, US Joint Chiefs of Staff, Institute for Policy Studies, *Europa Yearbook,* Center on Budget and Policy Priorities, Congressional Research Service (CRS), US General Accounting Office, ACCESS, Defense Budget Project, Research Project on National Income in East Central Europe.

Nuclear
US Department of Energy, Stockholm International Peace Research Institute (SIPRI), US Department of Defense, US Department of State, *Nuclear News,* International Atomic Energy Agency, Union of Concerned Scientists, Nuclear Control Institute, *The Bulletin of the Atomic Scientists, Nuclear Engineering International,* Institute for Policy Studies, Natural Resources Defense Council (NRDC), Federation of American Scientists.

Prices
World Bank, International Monetary Fund (IMF), US Department of Commerce.

Research and Development
National Science Foundation, Statistical Office of the European Communities, Organization for Economic Cooperation and Development.

*In addition to the sources named, data have been obtained from the regional commissions of the UN and from national statistical services.

References for
Estimates of Soviet Military Expenditures: A Critique (pages 62–63)

1. The arguments presented above are documented in: Franklyn D. Holzman, "Politics and Guesswork: CIA and DIA Estimates of Soviet Military Spending," *International Security,* Fall 1989.
2. D. Derk Swain, "The Soviet Military Sector: How it is Defined and Measured," in Henry S. Rowen and Charles Wolf, Jr. (editors), *The Improverished Superpower,* San Francisco: ICS Press, 1989, page 103, Figure 3.1.
3. For example, CIA published estimates comparing US and Soviet GNPs for the year 1987; Soviet GNP was 41 percent of US GNP with both valued in rubles and 69 percent with both valued in dollars.
4. Swain, p. 104.
5. This hypothesis is presented in Holzman, 1989, pp. 118–126.
6. The Soviet Government announced a separate figure of 3.9 billion rubles for military space programs. It is not clear whether the 77.3 billion ruble figure for total military expenditures includes these expenditures.
7. Anders Aslund, "How Small is Soviet National Income?" and Richard E. Ericson, "The Soviet Statistical Debate: Khanin versus TsSU" in Henry Rowen and Charles Wolf, Jr. (editors) *The Improverished Superpower,* San Francisco: ICS Press, 1989.
8. CIA has responded to revisionist criticisms in two studies published by the U.S. Directorate of Intelligence: *The Impact of Gorbachev's Policies on Soviet Economic Statistics,* SOV 88-10049, July, 1988; and *Revisiting Soviet Economic Performance under Glasnost': Implications for CIA Estimates,* SOV 88-10068, Sept. 1988.
9. V.D. Belkin of the Academy of Sciences and 6 other economists, "On the Burden of Military Expenditures"—an open letter. (Unfortunately, my photostat of the original Russian letter has the source and date torn off.)
10. S.Y. Blagovolin, "Geopolitical Aspects of Defense Sufficiency," *Kommunist,* #4, March 1990.

The statistics which follow have been assembled for the purpose of analyzing comparative progress on a broad front, primarily for the world as a whole or for groups of countries. It is believed that they are representative for this purpose.

Because of the interest in the national figures which make up these totals, we are showing them in full detail for 1987 (Table II). It cannot be emphasized too strongly that caution must be exercised in drawing conclusions from individual national figures, and particularly in making comparisons between countries. Some of the reasons why this is so are outlined in the statistical notes following.

Table III shows the country rank on a per capita basis for indicators of economic and social development including, for this special edition, selected environment indicators, both per capita and total. It is hoped that the selection is large enough to offset some of the inconsistencies in the individual series and to convey a general impression of relative standing.

MILITARY AND SOCIAL TRENDS
World, Developed,[1] and Developing[2] Countries, 1960, 1970, 1980, 1986–88

TABLE I

Military

	1960	1970	1980	1986	1987	1988	1960	1970	1980	1986	1987	1988	1960	1970	1980	1986	1987	1988
	Public Expenditures[3,4] billion 1987 US $						Public Expenditures[3,4] % of GNP						Public Expenditures[3,4] 1987 US $ per capita					
World	413	610	745	916	926	923	6.2	5.6	4.8	5.2	5.1	4.9	131	158	171	190	189	185
Developed	385	550	635	777	787	789	6.5	5.7	4.8	5.2	5.1	4.9	379	492	580	684	688	686
Developing	28	60	110	139	139	134	3.9	4.7	5.3	5.4	5.2	4.8	15	25	34	38	37	35
	Armed Forces thousands						Armed Forces population per soldier						Public Expenditures[3,4] per soldier, 1987 US $					
World	18,550	21,484	25,101	25,748	26,620	26,656	154	167	176	191	188	191	20,076	26,039	29,687	35,635	34,277	34,614
Developed	10,151	10,428	10,157	10,115	10,246	10,149	90	97	108	112	112	113	33,905	47,661	62,516	76,866	76,810	77,722
Developing	8,399	11,056	14,944	15,633	16,374	16,507	232	233	223	241	235	238	3,362	5,646	7,374	8,926	8,475	8,112

Health

	1960	1970	1980	1986	1987	1988	1960	1970	1980	1986	1987	1988	1960	1970	1980	1986	1987	1988
	Public Expenditures[4] billion 1987 US $						Public Expenditures[4] % of GNP						Public Expenditures[4] 1987 US $ per capita					
World	143	341	625	759	794	824	2.2	3.1	4.0	4.3	4.4	4.4	50	97	144	157	162	162
Developed	136	325	592	719	751	781	2.3	3.4	4.5	4.8	4.8	4.8	150	322	541	632	657	679
Developing	7	16	33	40	43	43	1.0	1.3	1.5	1.6	1.6	1.5	4	6	10	11	11	11
	Physicians thousands						Life Expectancy years						Infant Mortality rate per 1000 births					
World	1,588	2,233	3,936	4,913	5,025	5,130	55	60	63	64	65	65	118	93	79	72	71	70
Developed	1,182	1,620	2,508	3,011	3,080	3,140	70	71	73	73	74	74	30	21	16	14	14	14
Developing	406	613	1,428	1,902	1,945	1,990	48	56	60	61	62	63	136	106	89	80	79	78

Education

	1960	1970	1980	1986	1987	1988	1960	1970	1980	1986	1987	1988	1960	1970	1980	1986	1987	1988
	Public Expenditures[4] billion 1987 US $						Public Expenditures[4] % of GNP						Public Expenditures[4] 1987 US $ per capita					
World	235	510	779	878	903	928	3.5	4.6	5.1	5.0	5.0	4.9	80	142	180	183	185	182
Developed	218	469	697	780	803	824	3.7	4.9	5.3	5.2	5.2	5.1	240	464	636	686	703	717
Developing	17	41	82	98	100	104	2.3	3.1	3.7	3.8	3.8	3.7	9	16	25	27	27	26
	Teachers thousands						Student Enrollment millions in general education						Public Expenditures per student, 1987 US $					
World	14,631	21,535	32,056	35,948	36,710	37,130	405	593	775	833	841	852	591	879	1,026	1,073	1,094	1,089
Developed	6,795	9,000	10,203	10,523	10,731	10,840	158	187	176	173	173	173	1,378	2,510	3,969	4,512	4,645	4,763
Developing	7,836	12,535	21,853	25,425	25,979	26,290	247	406	599	660	668	679	72	104	141	151	154	153

Population

	1960	1970	1980	1986	1987	1988	1960	1970	1980	1986	1987	1988	1960	1970	1980	1986	1987	1988
	Population million						Population % distribution						Total Fertility Rate births per woman					
World	3,008	3,683	4,433	4,919	5,005	5,092	100	100	100	100	100	100	5.0	4.5	3.7	3.5	3.5	3.5
Developed	909	1,011	1,095	1,137	1,144	1,150	30.2	27.5	24.7	23.1	22.9	22.6	2.7	2.2	1.9	1.9	1.9	1.9
Developing	2,099	2,672	3,338	3,782	3,861	3,942	69.8	72.5	75.3	76.9	77.1	77.4	6.0	5.4	4.2	4.0	4.0	4.0

GNP

	1960	1970	1980	1986	1987	1988	1960	1970	1980	1986	1987	1988	1960	1970	1980	1986	1987	1988
	GNP[4] billion 1987 US $						GNP[4] % distribution						GNP per capita[4] 1987 US $					
World	6,675	10,968	15,436	17,678	18,227	18,905	100	100	100	100	100	100	2,242	3,002	3,508	3,608	3,655	3,726
Developed	5,927	9,646	13,157	15,086	15,526	16,090	88.8	87.9	85.2	85.3	85.2	8.51	6,520	9,540	12,015	13,264	13,576	13,995
Developing	748	1,322	2,279	2,592	2,701	2,815	11.2	12.1	14.8	14.7	14.8	14.9	361	500	689	689	703	717

Aid and Trade

	1960	1970	1980	1986	1987	1988	1960	1970	1980	1986	1987	1988	1960	1970	1980	1986	1987	1988
	Economic Aid Given billion US $						Arms Imports billion US $						Arms Exports billion US $					
World	5.1	8.6	40.0	46.9	50.4	55.7	2.4	5.9	35.0	46.9	53.7	48.1	2.4	5.8	35.5	46.0	54.3	48.9
Developed	5.0	7.9	29.9	41.5	46.6	53.1	1.3	2.0	8.2	12.7	13.6	13.6	2.3	5.6	34.1	43.2	49.9	43.5
Developing	.1	.7	10.1	5.4	3.8	2.6	1.1	3.9	26.8	34.2	40.1	34.5	.1	.2	1.4	2.8	4.4	5.4

1. *Developed countries,* 29 in number, are those identified by a small ■ in Tables II and III. They include countries listed in North America, most of Europe, Oceania, Israel, and Japan.

2. *Developing countries,* 113 in number, are the countries listed in Latin America, six in Europe (Albania, Greece, Malta, Portugal, Turkey and Yugoslavia), Asia except Israel and Japan, all of Africa, Fiji and Papua New Guinea in Oceania.

3. Data for Afghanistan, Cambodia, Equatorial Guinea, Laos, Lebanon, and Vietnam are not available for many years during the period shown.

4. Values expressed in 1987 prices and in general converted to dollars at 1987 exchange rates. Percentages and per capita data have been calculated before rounding and adjusted for any differences between series in available country coverage; therefore they may not agree exactly with averages calculated from the aggregates shown on this table.

5. Primary and secondary grades.

	HUMAN RESOURCES								GNP		PUBLIC EXPENDITURES											
	Population		Armed Forces		Teachers		Physicians				Military				Education				Health			
	thousand		thousand		thousand		thousand		million 1987 US dollars		million 1987 US dollars		% of GNP[1]		million 1987 US dollars		% of GNP[1]		million 1987 US dollars		% of GNP[1]	
	1960	1987	1960	1987	1960	1987	1960	1987	1960	1987	1960	1987	1960	1987	1960	1987	1960	1987	1960	1987	1960	1987
WORLD	3,007,578	5,004,854	18,550	26,620	14,631	36,710	1,587.8	5,024.6	6,674,657	18,226,744	412,645	925,761	6.2	5.1	235,493	903,653	3.5	5.0	143,235	794,028	2.2	4.4
■ Developed	909,108	1,143,610	10,151	10,246	6,795	10,731	1,182.1	3,079.5	5,926,958	15,525,964	384,621	786,990	6.5	5.1	217,982	803,437	3.7	5.2	136,143	751,076	2.3	4.8
Developing	2,098,470	3,861,244	8,399	16,374	7,836	25,979	405.7	1,945.1	747,699	2,700,780	28,024	138,771	3.9	5.2	17,511	100,216	2.3	3.8	7,092	42,952	1.0	1.6
AMERICA																						
North America	198,580	269,311	2,596	2,243	1,762	2,578	279.1	625.3	2,087,050	4,928,729	177,983	302,046	8.5	6.1	78,705	270,088	3.8	5.5	28,238	233,948	1.4	4.7
■ United States	180,671	243,441	2,476	2,158	1,600	2,296	259.4	570.0	1,959,435	4,526,700	172,550	293,211	8.8	6.5	73,479	240,820	3.8	5.3	25,232	207,300	1.3	4.6
■ Canada	17,909	25,870	120	85	162	282	19.7	55.3	127,615	402,029	5,433	8,835	4.3	2.2	5,226	29,268	4.1	7.3	3,006	26,648	2.4	6.6
Latin America	213,520	415,168	741	1,343	928	3,673	113.3	426.2	231,591	732,166	4,305	11,889	1.9	1.6	4,876	23,486	2.1	3.2	2,885	13,216	1.2	1.8
Argentina	20,616	31,138	127	78	153	364	27.8	81.0	42,563	76,846	902	1,145	2.1	1.5	851	1,445	2.0	1.9	298	1,180	.7	1.5
Barbados	231	256	—	—	1	3	.1	.2	536	1,430	•••	8	•••	.5	14	86	2.6	6.0	16	58	3.0	4.0
Bolivia	3,428	6,730	18	28	17	56	.9	4.2	1,906	3,725	39	175	2.0	4.7	29	108	1.5	2.9	8	15	.4	.4
Brazil	72,595	141,459	180	296	284	1,199	27.2	123.6	62,050	291,850	1,136	2,919	1.8	1.0	1,160	9,923	1.9	3.4	372	4,903	.6	1.7
Chile	7,614	12,537	42	98	24	101	4.3	9.9	8,479	17,374	233	575	2.8	3.3	229	823	2.7	4.7	170	357	2.0	2.1
Colombia	15,538	29,943	55	66	58	222	6.0	25.0	9,792	33,871	115	273	1.2	.8	169	905	1.7	2.7	37	237	.4	.7
Costa Rica[2]	1,236	2,791	—	—	9	17	.5	2.7	1,312	4,242	15	25	1.2	.6	54	189	4.1	4.5	39	212	3.0	5.0
Cuba	7,028	10,075	80	176	35	142	6.6	22.1	10,648	18,000	544	1,296	5.1	7.2	426	1,116	4.0	6.2	319	540	3.0	3.0
Dominican Rep.	3,231	6,716	19	21	10	42	.4	3.8	1,410	4,631	70	50	5.0	1.1	29	67	2.1	1.4	18	80	1.3	1.7
Ecuador	4,413	9,922	26	37	19	94	1.7	11.5	2,906	9,766	69	208	2.4	2.1	55	340	1.9	3.5	12	181	.4	1.9
El Salvador	2,570	4,927	6	47	10	25	.5	1.7	2,094	4,556	23	177	1.1	3.9	49	98	2.3	2.1	19	42	.9	.9
Guatemala	3,964	8,433	7	40	12	44	.7	3.6	2,403	6,868	22	124	1.4	1.8	33	154	1.4	2.2	14	85	.6	1.2
Guyana	569	989	—	5	4	6	.1	.1	212	247	•••	29	•••	11.8	6	24	3.0	9.6	5	11	2.2	4.4
Haiti	3,675	6,146	5	8	7	31	.4	.8	1,420	2,148	34	28	2.4	1.3	20	42	1.4	1.9	14	28	1.0	1.3
Honduras	1,935	4,680	6	17	8	25	.2	3.0	1,344	3,800	16	190	1.2	5.0	29	188	2.2	4.9	13	125	1.0	3.3
Jamaica	1,629	2,409	—	2	6	21	.6	1.2	1,831	2,528	•••	25	•••	1.0	42	132	2.3	5.2	37	71	2.0	2.8
Mexico	38,019	83,040	60	134	137	795	20.2	76.5	33,219	134,175	216	461	.6	.3	397	2,777	1.2	2.1	631	3,086	1.9	2.3
Nicaragua	1,493	3,502	5	77	5	22	.5	2.5	1,503	2,959	29	592	1.9	20.0	22	183	1.5	6.2	6	148	.4	5.0
Panama	1,148	2,274	—	5	7	23	.4	2.3	1,193	5,128	1	105	.1	2.0	43	276	3.6	5.4	36	295	3.0	5.7
Paraguay	1,774	3,923	19	17	12	37	1.0	2.5	1,112	4,336	19	49	1.7	1.1	15	56	1.3	1.3	6	13	.5	.3
Peru	9,931	20,727	46	113	49	188	5.1	18.8	15,613	43,686	317	2,184	2.0	5.0	351	1,477	2.3	3.4	172	371	1.1	.8
Trinidad & Tobago	843	1,223	—	2	6	13	.4	1.2	2,153	4,302	•••	43	•••	1.0	60	245	2.8	5.7	37	138	1.7	3.2
Uruguay	2,538	3,058	15	27	15	28	2.7	5.9	4,700	7,458	67	158	1.4	2.1	134	227	2.9	3.0	47	75	1.0	1.0
Venezuela	7,502	18,270	25	49	40	175	5.0	22.1	21,192	48,240	438	1,050	2.1	2.2	659	2,605	3.1	5.4	559	965	2.6	2.0
EUROPE																						
NATO Europe	308,091	376,445	3,350	3,262	1,708	3,363	286.8	772.3	1,825,804	4,422,501	83,242	148,339	4.6	3.4	54,831	213,887	3.0	4.8	49,709	254,911	2.7	5.8
■ Belgium	9,153	9,918	120	91	70	122	11.4	31.7	60,142	141,767	2,017	4,163	3.4	2.9	2,758	7,298	4.6	5.1	1,242	7,955	2.1	5.6
■ Denmark	4,581	5,120	44	29	29	71	5.7	13.1	45,656	97,086	1,258	2,141	2.8	2.2	1,454	7,713	3.2	7.9	1,504	5,175	3.3	5.3
■ France	45,684	55,596	781	547	288	531	44.6	138.8	329,622	878,767	20,898	34,859	6.3	4.0	7,846	49,211	2.4	5.6	8,028	56,025	2.4	6.4
■ Germany, West	55,433	60,812	270	488	238	484	79.4	171.5	500,490	1,124,012	20,011	34,135	4.0	3.0	13,785	49,455	2.8	4.4	15,857	70,619	3.2	6.3
Greece	8,327	9,992	158	209	32	82	10.4	33.3	13,476	46,712	643	2,902	4.8	6.2	201	1,261	1.5	2.7	245	1,868	1.8	4.0
■ Iceland	176	246	—	—	2	3	.2	.7	1,466	5,202	—	—	—	—	44	224	3.0	4.3	35	374	2.4	7.2
■ Italy	50,200	57,238	400	388	337	616	22.7	63.9	281,758	750,787	7,458	18,354	2.6	2.4	9,086	30,033	3.2	4.0	7,815	43,292	2.8	5.8
■ Luxembourg	314	367	3	1	2	3	.3	.7	2,692	8,102	27	73	1.0	.9	87	325	3.2	4.0	16	409	.6	5.1
■ Netherlands	11,480	14,595	135	108	65	136	12.8	34.6	88,817	213,170	3,463	6,543	3.9	3.1	4,020	15,994	4.5	7.5	1,154	13,326	1.3	6.3
■ Norway	3,581	4,177	40	37	30	57	4.3	9.5	27,512	82,329	878	2,753	3.2	3.3	1,116	5,512	4.1	6.7	706	6,018	2.6	7.3
Portugal	8,826	10,225	79	66	32	126	7.1	26.4	10,745	35,765	447	1,131	4.2	3.2	197	1,563	1.8	4.4	97	1,434	.9	4.0
■ Spain	30,455	38,910	300	325	112	301	35.7	131.2	84,506	286,731	2,472	6,906	2.9	2.4	972	9,134	1.1	3.2	1,013	12,420	1.2	4.3
Turkey	27,509	52,510	500	654	79	319	8.2	38.8	16,058	66,017	828	2,890	5.2	4.4	417	1,083	2.6	1.6	128	970	.8	1.5
■ United Kingdom	52,372	56,739	520	319	392	512	44.0	78.1	363,193	686,054	22,842	31,489	6.3	4.6	12,848	35,081	3.5	5.1	11,869	35,026	3.3	5.1
ALL NATO (incl. US and Canada)	506,671	645,756	5,946	5,505	3,470	5,941	565.9	1,397.6	3,912,854	9,351,230	261,225	450,385	6.7	4.8	133,536	483,975	3.4	5.2	77,947	488,859	2.0	5.2
Warsaw Pact	311,048	393,937	4,413	5,010	2,434	3,751	498.0	1,477.3	1,281,682	3,124,207	113,465	296,947	8.9	9.5	56,308	156,217	4.4	5.0	42,037	97,766	3.3	3.1
■ Bulgaria	7,867	8,985	100	153	51	72	11.1	27.1	20,748	51,734	665	1,966	3.2	3.8	535	2,586	2.6	5.0	415	1,868	2.0	3.6
■ Czechoslovakia	13,654	15,563	150	201	93	109	22.0	47.6	68,769	131,815	2,613	4,614	3.8	3.5	2,338	4,763	3.4	3.6	1,994	5,653	2.9	4.3
■ Germany, East	17,240	16,641	65	176	82	163	14.6	39.6	87,886	178,866	1,758	8,049	2.0	4.5	3,515	6,879	4.0	3.8	1,933	4,680	2.2	2.6
■ Hungary	9,984	10,607	75	106	63	100	13.9	35.4	35,057	68,198	631	1,432	1.8	2.1	1,122	2,476	3.2	3.6	911	2,017	2.6	3.0
■ Poland	29,561	37,743	200	394	160	353	27.6	77.3	76,652	171,471	2,323	4,801	3.0	2.8	2,913	7,636	3.8	4.5	2,683	7,043	3.5	4.1
■ Romania	18,407	22,936	200	180	101	147	23.4	48.3	42,570	112,123	975	1,345	2.3	1.2	1,235	1,737	2.9	1.5	851	1,795	2.0	1.6
■ USSR	214,335	281,462	3,623	3,800	1,884	2,807	385.4	1,202.0	950,000	2,410,000	104,500	274,740	11.0	11.4	44,650	130,140	4.7	5.4	33,250	74,710	3.5	3.1

	HUMAN RESOURCES								GNP		PUBLIC EXPENDITURES											
	Population		Armed Forces		Teachers		Physicians				Military				Education				Health			
	thousand		thousand		thousand		thousand		million 1987 US dollars		million 1987 US dollars		% of GNP[1]		million 1987 US dollars		% of GNP[1]		million 1987 US dollars		% of GNP[1]	
	1960	1987	1960	1987	1960	1987	1960	1987	1960	1987	1960	1987	1960	1987	1960	1987	1960	1987	1960	1987	1960	1987
Other Europe...	47,496	57,742	469	447	281	479	40.2	111.1	271,378	630,706	6,707	13,806	2.5	2.2	9,534	36,908	3.5	5.9	7,293	39,260	2.7	6.2
Albania.......	1,611	3,077	21	42	9	30	.4	4.5	1,390	3,600	125	151	9.0	4.2	...	...	...	...	...	83	...	2.3
■ Austria.......	7,048	7,494	38	55	38	86	9.6	14.5	47,744	116,264	555	1,447	1.2	1.2	1,364	6,903	2.9	5.9	1,469	6,592	3.1	5.7
■ Finland.......	4,430	4,937	45	34	29	47	2.8	11.0	32,068	87,705	529	1,458	1.7	1.7	1,507	5,165	4.7	5.9	682	5,208	2.1	5.9
■ Ireland.......	2,834	3,616	6	14	20	36	3.0	5.0	11,278	26,479	157	435	1.4	1.6	347	1,902	3.1	7.2	331	1,901	2.9	7.2
Malta........	329	345	—	1	2	4	.3	.5	335	1,680	...	21	...	1.3	13	61	3.8	3.6	10	60	3.0	3.6
■ Sweden......	7,480	8,349	80	67	64	72	7.1	22.5	73,821	155,969	2,043	4,433	2.8	2.8	3,154	11,581	4.3	7.4	2,521	13,209	3.4	8.5
■ Switzerland...	5,362	6,502	29	20	30	31	5.6	9.9	86,418	178,558	2,089	3,152	2.4	1.8	2,723	8,553	3.2	4.8	1,694	8,928	2.0	5.0
Yugoslavia....	18,402	23,422	250	214	89	173	11.4	43.2	18,324	60,451	1,209	2,709	6.6	4.5	426	2,743	2.3	4.5	586	3,279	3.2	5.4
ASIA																						
Middle East ...	74,266	168,924	587	2,986	256	1,597	25.7	141.3	89,378	366,116	5,017	61,708	5.6	16.9	3,245	18,265	3.6	5.0	692	6,884	.8	1.9
Bahrain	156	464	—	3	1	5	.1	.6	...	4,300	...	207	...	4.8	...	192	...	4.5	...	111	...	2.6
Cyprus.......	573	680	1	13	4	5	.4	.9	...	3,704	...	35	.5	.9	...	133	2.4	3.6	...	72	.6	2.0
Egypt[3].......	25,922	50,150	120	445	95	409	10.1	62.4	6,771	28,670	375	2,339	5.5	8.2	278	1,704	4.1	5.9	37	327	.6	1.1
Iran.........	20,301	51,310	200	654	54	477	5.3	16.9	42,296	92,000	1,916	19,000	4.5	20.7	1,004	2,650	2.4	2.9	338	1,380	.8	1.5
Iraq.........	6,847	17,053	80	1,000	29	160	1.3	9.5	15,474	31,000	1,346	9,370	8.7	30.2	902	1,429	5.8	4.6	155	248	1.0	.8
■ Israel	2,114	4,372	65	141	21	67	5.2	9.8	7,228	36,487	212	5,838	2.9	16.0	578	2,383	8.0	6.5	72	661	1.0	1.8
Jordan.......	1,695	3,790	35	80	9	38	.3	3.1	624	4,665	104	617	16.7	13.2	19	227	3.0	4.9	4	125	.6	2.7
Kuwait	278	1,860	—	15	2	30	.2	2.8	...	25,761	...	1,335	1.5	5.2	...	1,374	2.8	5.3	...	721	...	2.8
Lebanon	1,857	2,762	8	16	11	44	1.5	3.0	...	...	...	...	1.7	...	...	...	1.1	...	...	...	...	...
Oman........	505	1,334	—	22	1	13	<.1	1.2	389	7,294	...	1,518	...	20.8	...	390	...	5.3	...	164	...	2.2
Qatar........	45	326	—	7	1	6	<.1	.7	...	4,206	...	154	...	3.7	...	279	4.2	6.5	...	...	...	...
Saudi Arabia..	4,075	12,563	25	74	6	144	.2	18.0	10,940	75,000	619	16,500	5.7	22.0	348	5,565	3.2	7.4	66	2,663	.6	3.6
Syria........	4,561	11,229	52	408	20	135	1.0	8.6	5,656	23,751	445	2,721	7.9	11.5	116	1,109	2.1	4.7	20	104	.4	.4
United Arab Emir.	90	1,453	—	43	...	16	...	1.9	...	23,695	...	1,580	...	6.7	...	520	...	2.2	...	237	...	1.0
Yemen, Arab Rep.	4,039	7,309	1	37	1	33	<.1	1.3	...	4,643	...	306	...	6.6	...	254	...	5.5	...	47	...	1.0
Yemen, People's Dem. Rep.	1,208	2,269	—	28	1	15	.1	.6	...	940	...	188	...	20.0	...	56	...	6.0	...	24	...	2.5
South Asia ...	573,788	1,068,933	1,008	1,947	2,033	5,179	102.6	376.9	104,244	311,191	2,096	12,918	2.2	4.2	2,299	10,201	2.2	3.3	496	2,573	.5	.8
Afghanistan ..	10,775	14,709	100	50	5	22	.3	2.5	...	...	...	...	2.2	...	...	...	2.2	...	...	...	...	...
Bangladesh...	51,419	106,702	—	102	105	301	...	16.2	7,246	17,482	...	291	...	1.7	45	345	.6	2.0	...	105	...	.6
India........	442,346	802,134	775	1,262	1,761	4,317	91.5	306.0	86,963	251,669	1,704	9,815	2.0	3.9	2,098	8,808	2.4	3.5	435	2,265	.5	.9
Nepal........	9,404	17,788	20	30	6	75	.1	.9	1,259	2,741	5	33	.4	1.2	5	77	.4	2.8	2	23	.2	.8
Pakistan......	49,955	111,036	103	481	84	320	8.5	49.0	6,731	32,647	367	2,575	5.4	7.9	74	726	1.1	2.2	18	65	.3	.2
Sri Lanka.....	9,889	16,564	10	22	72	144	2.2	2.3	2,045	6,652	20	204	1.0	3.1	77	245	3.8	3.7	41	115	2.0	1.7
Far East......	1,012,152	1,691,970	5,127	7,741	4,666	13,284	208.3	970.5	574,185	3,162,711	16,742	57,677	5.9	4.6	20,714	143,847	3.6	4.6	8,886	129,485	1.6	4.1
Brunei.......	84	241	—	4	1	3	...	.2	...	3,195	...	285	...	8.9	...	133	...	4.2	...	26	...	.8
Burma	21,746	39,141	90	186	47	158	1.4	11.1	3,966	10,083	277	190	7.0	1.9	88	198	2.2	2.0	28	73	.7	.7
Cambodia	5,433	7,683	30	50	15	28	.2	.5	1,351	1,207	73	...	5.4	...	47	...	3.5	...	18	...	1.3	...
China........	646,283	1,068,802	2,000	3,200	3,000	8,304	81.0	640.0	60,005	304,962	7,201	13,418	12.0	4.4	1,080	8,235	1.8	2.7	780	4,269	1.3	1.4
Indonesia	96,194	172,185	375	284	264	1,919	1.9	21.5	15,417	65,077	889	1,367	5.8	2.1	965	2,197	.6	3.4	40	335	.3	.5
■ Japan........	94,096	121,910	206	246	740	994	96.0	191.3	430,816	2,387,292	4,416	24,198	1.0	1.0	17,065	119,367	4.0	5.0	7,810	120,315	1.8	5.0
Korea, North..	10,526	21,389	340	838	40	—	3.5	...	5,261	25,000	579	2,500	11.0	10.0	...	...	...	...	26	250	.5	1.0
Korea, South..	25,003	42,119	600	629	81	250	7.1	33.5	14,589	128,415	881	6,125	6.0	4.8	655	5,035	4.5	3.9	29	484	.2	.4
Laos.........	2,177	3,779	55	56	3	30	<.1	.6	215	538	12	...	5.8	...	...	3	...	.6	1	...	.5	...
Malaysia	8,140	16,191	22	113	50	159	1.2	5.9	5,534	29,654	102	1,335	1.9	4.5	152	2,042	2.7	6.9	59	446	1.1	1.5
Mongolia	931	2,027	18	34	2	18	.9	5.2	648	1,580	27	172	4.2	10.9	...	...	...	...	...	22	...	1.4
Philippines ...	27,561	57,997	32	105	139	360	3.9	8.7	10,860	34,144	126	609	1.2	1.8	248	675	2.3	2.0	43	240	.4	.7
Singapore	1,634	2,616	—	56	11	20	.7	2.9	2,384	20,742	9	1,059	.4	5.1	67	1,047	2.8	5.0	24	260	1.0	1.3
Taiwan	11,209	19,768	600	424	53	155	6.0	19.4	9,520	89,000	1,228	4,762	12.9	5.4	191	3,204	2.7	3.6	...	2,225	...	2.5
Thailand	26,392	53,314	134	256	122	453	3.4	9.5	7,326	47,322	173	1,657	2.4	3.5	156	1,711	2.1	3.6	28	540	.4	1.1
Vietnam......	34,743	62,808	625	1,260	98	433	1.1	20.2	6,293	14,500	749	...	11.9	...	...	...	...	...	...	...	...	...
Oceania	15,001	23,882	60	90	100	255	14.9	39.8	84,761	214,327	1,848	5,688	2.2	2.7	2,253	11,517	2.7	5.4	2,054	12,025	2.5	5.6
■ Australia	10,315	16,162	47	70	72	198	12.0	33.2	64,228	177,054	1,575	4,830	2.5	2.7	1,793	9,330	2.8	5.3	1,553	9,816	2.4	5.5
Fiji.........	394	715	—	3	2	7	.2	.4	415	1,119	...	26	...	2.3	12	71	2.8	6.4	4	27	1.0	2.4
■ New Zealand .	2,372	3,302	13	13	20	35	2.6	5.9	19,100	33,213	273	790	1.4	2.4	422	1,968	2.2	5.9	497	2,093	2.6	6.3
Papua New Guinea	1,920	3,703	—	4	6	15	.1	.3	1,018	2,941	...	42	...	1.4	26	148	2.5	5.0	...	89	...	3.0

	HUMAN RESOURCES								GNP		PUBLIC EXPENDITURES											
	Population		Armed Forces		Teachers		Physicians				Military				Education				Health			
	thousand		thousand		thousand		thousand		million 1987 US dollars		million 1987 US dollars		% of GNP[1]		million 1987 US dollars		% of GNP[1]		million 1987 US dollars		% of GNP[1]	
	1960	1987	1960	1987	1960	1987	1960	1987	1960	1987	1960	1987	1960	1987	1960	1987	1960	1987	1960	1987	1960	1987
AFRICA	253,636	538,542	199	1,551	463	2,551	18.9	83.9	124,584	334,090	1,240	14,743	1.2	4.4	2,728	19,237	2.2	5.8	945	3,960	.8	1.2
Sub-Sahara Africa[4]	208,244	447,409	109	963	330	1,734	7.3	37.2	65,172	144,102	390	6,007	.8	4.2	1,105	5,591	1.7	3.9	432	1,544	.8	1.1
• Other Africa	45,392	91,133	90	588	133	817	11.6	46.7	59,412	189,988	850	8,736	1.4	4.6	1,623	13,646	2.7	7.2	513	2,416	.9	1.3
• Algeria	10,800	23,102	—	169	25	241	1.9	10.2	19,374	61,956	397	1,196	2.0	1.9	425	6,199	2.2	10.0	232	817	1.2	1.3
Angola	4,816	9,226	—	53	3	23	.3	.5	8,146	10,200	...	2,040	...	20.0	28	306	.3	3.0	...	102	...	1.0
Benin	2,251	4,309	—	4	2	17	<.1	.3	804	1,710	9	31	1.1	1.8	20	86	2.5	5.0	12	14	1.5	.8
Botswana	481	1,157	—	3	1	10	<.1	.2	88	1,368	...	82	...	6.0	2	126	2.7	9.2	1	52	1.5	3.8
Burkina Faso	4,528	8,305	—	9	1	9	.1	.2	679	1,690	4	51	.6	3.0	10	50	1.5	3.0	4	17	.6	1.0
Burundi	2,927	5,002	—	7	3	10	<.1	.2	328	1,108	...	32	...	2.9	8	35	2.4	3.1	3	9	.8	.8
Cameroon	5,501	10,402	4	12	12	48	.2	.7	2,938	12,126	49	232	1.7	1.9	49	334	1.7	2.8	29	101	1.0	.8
Central African Rep.	1,605	2,703	—	4	1	6	<.1	.2	671	1,058	...	19	...	1.8	12	53	1.8	5.0	9	13	1.3	1.2
Chad	3,064	5,268	—	17	1	7	...	.1	656	702	...	34	...	4.9	6	14	.9	2.0	3	4	.5	.6
Congo	972	1,837	—	9	2	12	.1	.2	532	2,048	2	92	.3	4.5	13	111	2.5	5.4	9	43	1.6	2.1
Equatorial Guinea	252	410	—	1	<1	2	<.1	...	...	135	...	...	...	...	...	...	...	...	...	...	...	...
Ethiopia	24,192	43,850	25	320	7	77	.2	.6	2,266	5,372	36	472	1.6	8.8	19	225	.8	4.2	16	67	.7	1.3
Gabon	486	1,058	—	3	1	6	.1	.4	945	3,008	...	140	...	4.6	20	214	2.1	7.1	5	48	1.5	1.6
Gambia	353	789	—	1	...	3	<.1	.1	44	158	...	16	...	10.0	1	5	2.2	3.3	1	3	2.0	1.6
Ghana	6,774	13,704	10	11	22	117	.3	1.9	3,325	4,936	38	45	1.1	.9	127	169	3.8	3.4	35	58	1.1	1.2
Guinea	3,660	6,380	5	10	2	11	.1	.1	1,266	1,985	17	60	1.3	3.0	19	60	1.5	3.0	13	20	1.0	1.0
Ivory Coast	3,779	11,142	4	7	7	50	.1	.6	2,121	9,439	10	117	.5	1.2	97	566	4.6	6.0	32	159	1.5	1.7
Kenya	8,332	22,141	—	13	20	171	.8	2.3	1,785	7,669	3	237	.1	3.1	68	543	3.8	7.1	12	153	.7	2.0
Lesotho	870	1,628	—	—	3	8	<.1	.1	103	689	...	20	...	2.9	3	29	3.2	4.2	1	12	1.0	1.8
Liberia	1,037	2,321	2	6	2	7	.1	.2	652	1,063	7	26	1.1	2.4	4	43	.7	4.0	5	19	.8	1.8
• Libya	1,349	4,083	8	76	5	76	.2	5.6	4,331	23,810	51	2,956	1.2	12.4	119	2,255	2.8	9.5	56	762	1.3	3.2
Madagascar	5,309	10,886	2	21	8	53	.6	1.2	1,394	1,922	4	37	.3	1.9	33	56	2.3	2.9	20	38	1.4	2.0
Malawi	3,529	7,627	—	5	7	18	.1	.2	379	1,192	...	21	...	1.8	8	38	2.1	3.2	1	23	.2	1.9
Mali	4,636	8,569	2	7	2	13	.1	.3	641	1,865	11	61	1.7	3.3	13	62	2.0	3.3	6	14	1.0	.7
Mauritania	991	1,864	—	15	1	5	<.1	.2	347	869	...	40	...	4.6	7	50	2.1	5.8	2	17	.5	2.0
Mauritius	661	1,064	—	...	4	10	.1	.8	527	1,743	1	4	.2	.2	16	61	3.0	3.5	8	30	1.5	1.7
• Morocco	11,626	23,306	40	204	23	155	1.2	4.4	5,307	15,982	107	800	2.0	5.0	163	899	3.1	5.6	53	161	1.0	1.0
Mozambique	7,461	14,455	—	32	5	23	.3	.3	...	1,264	...	102	...	8.0	...	51	.4	4.0	...	23	...	1.8
Namibia	821	1,705	—	—	...	11	...	.3	...	1,800	...	...	...	...	17	54	...	3.0	...	11	...	.6
Niger	3,234	6,489	—	3	1	10	<.1	.2	1,540	2,085	4	17	.3	.8	7	67	.5	3.2	3	15	.2	.7
Nigeria	42,305	101,907	6	94	103	384	.7	14.2	12,239	23,352	22	180	.2	.8	90	349	.7	1.5	35	51	.3	.2
Rwanda	2,742	6,529	—	5	7	18	<.1	.2	821	2,142	...	38	...	1.8	3	74	.3	3.4	4	13	.5	.6
Senegal	3,041	6,791	4	10	3	18	.1	.5	2,290	4,374	11	96	.5	2.2	55	197	2.4	4.5	34	48	1.5	1.1
Sierra Leone	2,241	3,849	—	3	3	17	.1	.3	...	668	...	5	...	.8	...	9	...	1.3	...	4	...	.6
Somalia	2,935	6,865	4	65	1	11	.1	.5	517	967	...	23	...	2.4	5	6	.9	.6	3	2	.6	.2
• South Africa	17,396	33,016	24	97	70	278	7.9	22.8	28,000	79,123	243	3,292	.9	4.2	844	3,799	3.0	4.8	134	475	.5	.6
Sudan	11,165	23,128	18	58	11	75	.3	2.3	7,180	13,396	110	800	1.5	6.0	136	563	1.9	4.2	69	27	1.0	.2
Swaziland	326	712	—	—	1	6	<.1	.1	98	590	...	8	...	1.3	2	36	2.5	6.2	1	13	.8	2.3
Tanzania	10,026	24,488	—	40	11	101	.6	1.2	1,250	3,202	2	171	.1	5.3	26	116	2.1	3.6	7	35	.5	1.1
Togo	1,514	3,148	—	6	1	14	<.1	.2	385	1,198	...	43	...	3.6	7	78	1.9	6.5	5	20	1.3	1.7
• Tunisia	4,221	7,626	18	42	10	67	.4	3.7	2,400	9,117	52	492	2.2	5.4	72	494	3.0	5.4	38	201	1.6	2.2
Uganda	6,562	16,599	—	20	12	88	.5	.6	2,204	3,345	39	80	1.8	2.4	71	50	3.2	1.5	15	10	.7	.3
Zaire	15,908	32,698	18	26	40	152	.2	2.5	3,374	5,134	...	82	.3	1.6	79	139	2.4	2.7	...	44	...	.9
Zambia	3,141	7,563	—	16	6	35	.3	.9	1,018	1,741	11	63	1.1	3.6	16	60	1.6	3.5	10	34	1.0	2.0
Zimbabwe	3,816	8,841	5	47	13	78	.8	1.3	1,619	4,789	...	390	...	8.1	8	506	.5	10.6	19	178	1.2	3.7

■ Developed country   • Other Africa   — none or negligible   ... not available   <1 less than 1

1. Percent of GNP is computed before rounding and may not agree exactly with values shown on the table.

2. Costa Rica abolished its army in 1948; there is a paramilitary civil guard.

3. Egypt is shown with the political grouping of Middle East states, rather than in Africa.

4. Not including South Africa, which is included with "Other Africa."

	MILITARY						GNP		EDUCATION							
	Public Expenditures				Equivalent Years of Income[1]		Military Burden[2]	Economic-Social Standing[3]	per Capita		Public Expenditures per Capita		School-Age Population per Teacher[4]		School-Age Population in School[4]		Literacy Rate[5]		Education[6]
	Rank	% of GNP	Rank	per Capita	Rank	1,000 Years	Average Rank	Average Rank	Rank	US$	Rank	US$	Rank	No.	Rank	%	F Rank	F/M %	Average Rank
WORLD		5.1		189		225,374				3,655		185		33		70		65/79	
▪ Developed		5.1		688		64,644				13,576		703		18		89		98/99	
Developing		5.2		37		160,730				703		27		39		67		52/72	
AMERICA																			
North America		6.1		1,122		16,338				18,301		1,003		18		100		99/99	
▪ US	26	6.5	3	1,204	4	15,769	4	9	8	18,595	8	989	18	18	1	100	4	99/99	8
▪ Canada	85	2.2	25	342	46	569	49	4	13	15,540	5	1,131	8	16	1	100	4	99/99	5
Latin America		1.6		29		7,263				1,764		57		30		79		81/85	
Argentina	109	1.5	73	37	53	464	84	45	51	2,468	74	46	27	20	51	79	29	95/96	45
Barbados	132	0.5	79	31	134	1	129	27	36	5,586	32	334	27	20	1	100	19	98/99	20
Bolivia	41	4.7	82	26	64	316	61	96	97	553	101	16	68	33	51	79	79	65/84	75
Brazil	120	1.0	85	21	21	1,415	81	58	57	2,063	61	70	52	29	47	80	66	76/79	57
Chile	62	3.3	68	46	58	415	63	53	66	1,386	63	66	54	30	25	87	38	91/92	45
Colombia	127	0.8	105	9	73	241	114	74	74	1,131	86	30	74	35	61	76	48	87/89	67
Costa Rica	131	0.6	105	9	125	17	131	55	65	1,520	62	68	81	40	79	71	34	93/94	64
Cuba	23	7.2	45	129	40	725	22	42	61	1,787	53	111	7	15	51	79	26	96/96	34
Dominican Rep.	118	1.1	110	7	109	72	125	81	90	690	109	10	92	47	23	88	64	77/78	72
Ecuador	89	2.1	85	21	79	211	91	71	80	984	79	34	58	31	32	85	59	80/85	57
El Salvador	54	3.9	74	36	82	191	73	88	81	925	95	20	104	65	93	64	70	69/75	91
Guatemala	98	1.8	89	15	85	152	101	93	86	814	98	18	98	59	108	50	94	47/63	100
Guyana	11	11.8	81	29	94	117	61	92	119	250	92	24	85	43	75	72	29	95/97	70
Haiti	111	1.3	121	5	105	81	125	115	109	349	114	7	96	58	101	58	104	35/40	104
Honduras	35	5.0	72	41	75	234	58	84	87	812	75	40	95	55	85	70	87	58/61	86
Jamaica	120	1.0	104	10	122	24	129	61	79	1,049	69	55	70	34	39	82	26	96/96	51
Mexico	133	0.3	117	6	66	285	117	59	63	1,616	81	33	63	32	39	82	40	88/92	56
Nicaragua	5	20.0	40	169	42	700	14	77	84	845	70	52	89	45	75	72	40	88/88	69
Panama	93	2.0	68	46	118	47	103	50	54	2,255	49	121	52	29	64	75	40	88/89	51
Paraguay	118	1.1	93	12	120	44	124	79	77	1,105	103	14	54	30	89	67	52	85/91	75
Peru	35	5.0	51	105	33	1,036	25	63	56	2,108	60	71	63	32	15	91	62	78/92	50
Trinidad & Tobago	120	1.0	76	35	127	12	121	40	44	3,518	41	201	39	24	9	93	29	95/97	30
Uruguay	89	2.1	62	52	111	65	98	47	52	2,439	59	74	35	22	28	86	33	94/93	39
Venezuela	85	2.2	60	57	60	398	67	48	49	2,640	46	143	44	27	37	83	49	86/88	44
EUROPE																			
NATO Europe		3.4		394		13,229				11,748		568		20		80		93/97	
▪ Belgium	72	2.9	21	420	65	291	51	15	16	14,294	17	736	2	12	61	76	4	99/99	21
▪ Denmark	85	2.2	22	418	98	113	67	3	6	18,962	1	1,506	2	12	36	84	4	99/99	11
▪ France	53	4.0	11	627	14	2,205	12	10	12	15,806	13	885	18	18	25	87	4	99/99	15
▪ Germany, West	69	3.0	12	561	18	1,847	18	11	9	18,483	15	813	13	17	51	79	4	99/99	21
Greece	27	6.2	30	290	45	621	20	29	41	4,675	47	126	33	21	18	90	40	88/97	35
▪ Iceland		—		—		—		4	3	21,146	11	913	27	20	47	80	1	100/100	22
▪ Italy	78	2.4	26	321	22	1,399	28	25	19	13,117	25	525	13	17	95	63	26	96/98	40
▪ Luxembourg	124	0.9	36	199	132	3	109	1	2	22,076	12	887	•••		•••		1	100/100	3
▪ Netherlands	66	3.1	19	448	55	448	36	12	15	14,606	6	1,096	22	19	28	86	4	99/99	15
▪ Norway	62	3.3	10	659	88	140	51	2	4	19,710	3	1,320	4	13	44	81	1	100/100	13
Portugal	65	3.2	50	111	63	323	57	36	45	3,498	45	153	8	16	19	89	59	80/89	33
▪ Spain	78	2.4	39	177	35	937	46	21	30	7,369	37	235	40	25	19	89	37	92/97	33
Turkey	49	4.4	61	55	13	2,298	26	78	67	1,257	94	21	83	41	75	72	85	62/86	84
▪ United Kingdom	42	4.6	13	555	12	2,604	8	16	21	12,091	18	618	22	19	19	89	4	99/99	16
ALL NATO (incl. US & Canada)		4.8		697		29,567				14,481		749		19		88		96/98	
Warsaw Pact		9.5		754		35,277				7,931		397		18		87		98/99	
▪ Bulgaria	56	3.8	35	219	62	341	46	32	35	5,758	35	288	35	22	44	81	34	93/96	37
▪ Czechoslovakia	60	3.5	28	296	47	545	34	28	27	8,470	33	306	51	28	79	71	4	99/99	42
▪ Germany, East	45	4.5	17	484	37	749	18	20	23	10,749	29	413	13	17	67	74	4	99/99	28
▪ Hungary	89	2.1	43	135	76	223	69	33	32	6,430	38	233	22	19	79	71	19	98/99	40
▪ Poland	75	2.8	46	127	31	1,057	46	37	42	4,543	39	202	27	20	61	76	19	98/99	37
▪ Romania	114	1.2	59	59	69	275	88	46	39	4,889	58	76	58	31	89	67	29	95/98	59
▪ USSR	13	11.4	7	976	2	32,087	2	19	26	8,562	26	462	8	16	7	94	19	98/99	15

HEALTH / ENVIRONMENT

Public Expenditures per Capita Rank	US$	Population per Physician Rank	No.	Infant Mortality[7] Rank	Rate	Life Expectancy[8] Rank	Years	Health Average Rank[8]	Total Fertility Rate Rank	Rate per Woman[9]	Deforestation Rank	1000 Hectares[10]	Energy Consumption Rank	Kilos per Capita[11]	CO$_2$ Emissions Rank	Million Metric Tons[12]	Greenhouse Gas Emissions Rank	Million Metric Tons[13]	Environment Average Rank[14]	
	162		992		71		65			3.5		20,462		1,493		5,459.0		5,778.8		**WORLD**
	657		371		14		74			1.9		—		4,893		3,843.3		3,127.2		■ Developed
	11		1,974		79		62			4.0		20,462		495		1,615.7		2,651.6		Developing
																				AMERICA
	869		431		10		75			1.8				7,448		1,336.5		1,120.0		**North America**
14	852	18	427	18	10	15	75	16	20	1.8		...	135	7,275	139	1,225.6	138	1,000.0	135	■ US
8	1,030	23	468	8	8	2	77	10	7	1.6		...	137	9,078	131	111.0	127	120.0	133	■ Canada
	32		974		56		67			3.6		12,269		964		248.5		921.7		**Latin America**
53	38	11	384	55	32	41	71	40	49	3.0		...	92	1,471	111	30.7	107	31.0	111	Argentina
27	226	55	1,045	25	12	15	75	31	30	2.0		...	96	1,773	15	0.2	4	0.2	13	Barbados
115	2	72	1,602	113	110	105	53	101	98	6.0	52	117	55	258	52	1.1	56	4.4	64	Bolivia
56	35	59	1,144	76	63	67	65	65	55	3.4	78	9,050	79	825	122	53.8	136	610.0	120	Brazil
60	28	63	1,266	40	20	36	72	50	44	2.7	34	50	78	822	82	7.2	66	6.4	61	Chile
91	8	60	1,198	67	46	64	66	71	57	3.5	75	890	76	786	96	13.9	122	69.0	102	Colombia
47	76	54	1,034	35	18	15	75	38	52	3.2	55	124	67	542	40	0.7	71	7.8	51	Costa Rica
48	54	22	456	31	15	15	75	29	11	1.7	5	2	86	1,135	90	9.2	68	6.9	36	Cuba
78	12	74	1,767	78	65	64	66	74	62	3.8	11	4	58	335	64	1.8	37	2.4	28	Dominican Rep.
72	18	47	863	76	63	67	65	66	72	4.6	67	340	70	618	73	4.1	96	21.0	79	Ecuador
88	9	84	2,865	72	60	82	62	82	79	4.8	12	5	48	217	35	0.6	23	1.3	18	El Salvador
84	10	81	2,356	72	60	82	62	80	91	5.8	49	90	41	169	46	0.9	61	5.1	53	Guatemala
80	11	99	6,965	60	40	60	68	75	46	2.8	9	3	62	471	24	0.3	11	0.4	7	Guyana
102	5	105	7,683	117	117	97	55	105	74	4.7	5	2	19	50	15	0.2	9	0.3	4	Haiti
63	27	70	1,560	81	69	71	64	71	83	5.5	49	90	43	192	31	0.5	63	5.2	43	Honduras
59	29	78	2,095	35	18	25	74	49	47	2.9	5	2	80	838	62	1.6	21	1.2	22	Jamaica
55	37	57	1,085	58	47	55	69	59	59	3.6	73	615	89	1,282	127	81.1	126	78.0	123	Mexico
52	42	68	1,401	75	62	78	63	68	83	5.5	54	121	54	256	35	0.6	73	8.4	59	Nicaragua
39	130	51	1,006	43	23	36	72	42	51	3.1	29	36	95	1,626	40	0.7	49	3.3	40	Panama
109	3	71	1,569	63	42	61	67	76	72	4.6	63	212	49	224	31	0.5	55	4.1	45	Paraguay
72	18	58	1,103	97	88	84	61	78	70	4.4	66	270	63	474	81	6.5	98	23.0	79	Peru
41	113	53	1,028	40	20	48	70	46	44	2.7	3	1	128	5,161	76	4.8	44	2.8	58	Trinidad & Tobago
67	24	29	518	53	27	41	71	48	42	2.6		...	74	761	46	0.9	41	2.5	34	Uruguay
49	53	45	827	58	36	48	70	50	62	3.8	64	245	103	2,394	109	26.7	103	27.0	109	Venezuela
																				EUROPE
	677		487		28		74			1.9		...		3,110		738.5		782.7		**NATO Europe**
15	802	5	313	18	10	15	75	13	7	1.6		...	124	4,844	109	26.7	99	25.0	98	■ Belgium
9	1,011	13	390	5	7	15	75	11	2	1.5		...	116	3,894	105	16.9	84	15.0	85	■ Denmark
10	1,008	15	400	8	8	9	76	11	20	1.8		...	114	3,731	129	94.7	127	120.0	129	■ France
5	1,161	8	355	8	8	15	75	9	1	1.4		...	120	4,560	135	181.5	132	160.0	125	■ Germany, West
31	187	4	300	29	13	9	76	18	11	1.7		...	99	1,970	104	16.1	94	20.0	86	Greece
2	1,515	9	370	1	5	2	77	4	34	2.1		...	133	6,882	31	0.5	11	0.4	38	■ Iceland
16	756	48	896	18	10	9	76	23	2	1.5		...	107	2,681	130	102.0	127	120.0	114	■ Italy
6	1,115	31	551	13	9	25	74	19	2	1.5		...		...	65	2.3	29	1.6	...	■ Luxembourg
12	913	17	422	8	8	2	77	10	2	1.5		...	129	5,223	115	36.4	115	43.0	112	■ Netherlands
3	1,441	19	440	5	7	2	77	7	11	1.7		...	136	8,959	94	12.2	75	8.7	91	■ Norway
37	140	12	388	31	15	30	73	28	11	1.7		...	90	1,325	88	8.4	90	17.0	73	Portugal
23	319	2	297	18	10	2	77	11	11	1.7		...	97	1,935	120	47.2	123	73.0	107	■ Spain
72	18	66	1,352	90	76	71	64	75	61	3.7		...	75	765	115	36.4	105	29.0	110	Turkey
18	617	40	726	13	9	15	75	22	20	1.8		...	115	3,818	134	157.2	131	150.0	131	■ United Kingdom
	757		462		20		75			1.9				4,949		2,075.1		1,902.7		**ALL NATO** (incl. US & Canada)
	248		267		22		70			2.3				4,763		1,435.8		919.0		**Warsaw Pact**
29	208	7	331	31	15	36	72	26	26	1.9		...	121	4,698	112	33.7	90	17.0	106	■ Bulgaria
22	363	6	327	29	13	41	71	25	30	2.0		...	125	4,957	125	65.3	108	33.0	125	■ Czechoslovakia
24	281	16	420	13	9	30	73	21	11	1.7		...	131	6,031	128	90.0	119	62.0	127	■ Germany, East
30	190	3	299	34	17	41	71	27	20	1.8		...	108	3,066	108	20.9	80	13.0	91	■ Hungary
31	187	26	488	35	18	41	71	33	35	2.2		...	110	3,378	132	127.7	124	76.0	132	■ Poland
46	78	24	475	42	22	48	70	40	35	2.2		...	111	3,465	123	58.0	104	28.0	119	■ Romania
45	265	1	234	45	24	48	70	30	38	2.4		...	126	5,035	138	1,040.2	137	690.0	136	■ USSR

| | MILITARY | | | | | | | Economic-Social Standing[3] | GNP per Capita | | EDUCATION | | | | | | Literacy Rate[5] | | Education[6] |
| | Public Expenditures | | | | Equivalent Years of Income[1] | | Military Burden[2] | | | | Public Expenditures per Capita | | School-Age Population per Teacher[4] | | School-Age Population in School[4] | | | | |
	Rank	% of GNP	Rank	per Capita	Rank	1,000 Years	Average Rank	Average Rank	Rank	US$	Rank	US$	Rank	No.	Rank	%	F Rank	F/M %	Average Rank
Other Europe		2.2		239		1,769				10,923		675		21		75		93/98	
Albania	51	4.2	66	49	92	129	73	56	71	1,170	•••		44	27	64	75		•••/•••	54
■ Austria	114	1.2	38	193	101	93	91	17	14	15,514	10	921	4	13	79	71	19	98/98	28
■ Finland	105	1.7	29	295	104	82	85	6	10	17,765	7	1,046	8	16	23	88	4	99/99	11
■ Ireland	107	1.6	47	120	112	59	100	22	31	7,323	24	526	38	23	15	91	4	99/99	20
Malta	111	1.3	58	61	131	4	111	38	40	4,870	43	175	27	20	39	82	57	82/86	42
■ Sweden	75	2.8	15	531	74	237	55	7	7	18,681	2	1,387	18	18	56	78	4	99/99	20
■ Switzerland	98	1.8	16	485	95	115	73	13	1	27,462	4	1,315	54	30	60	77	4	99/99	31
Yugoslavia	45	4.5	49	116	32	1,050	28	49	50	2,581	51	117	41	26	86	69	49	86/97	57
ASIA																			
Middle East		16.9		365		26,541				2,203		110		31		74		38/65	
Bahrain	39	4.8	20	447	123	22	58	35	25	9,267	28	414	33	21	15	91	82	64/79	40
Cyprus	124	0.9	64	51	130	6	119	31	38	5,447	42	196	22	19	12	92	40	88/95	29
Egypt	19	8.2	67	47	8	4,092	15	89	96	572	79	34	70	34	67	74	112	30/59	82
Iran	4	20.7	31	370	5	10,597	4	72	60	1,793	70	52	58	31	56	78	102	39/62	72
Iraq	1	30.2	14	549	7	5,154	2	72	59	1,818	57	84	70	34	67	74	100	41/75	74
■ Israel	8	16.0	1	1,335	42	700	6	23	28	8,346	23	545	8	16	39	82	34	93/97	26
Jordan	9	13.2	41	163	51	501	20	70	68	1,231	65	60	63	32	72	73	83	63/87	71
Kuwait	33	5.2	9	718	100	96	36	24	17	13,850	16	739	13	17	25	87	70	69/76	31
Lebanon		•••		•••		•••		41		•••		•••	18	18	28	86	70	69/86	29
Oman	3	20.8	5	1,138	68	278	11	65	37	5,468	34	292	58	31	79	71	129	12/47	75
Qatar	57	3.7	18	473	127	12	65	26	20	12,902	14	856	1	11	5	99	91	51/51	28
Saudi Arabia	2	22.0	2	1,313	11	2,764	1	52	33	5,970	27	443	41	26	100	59	108	31/71	69
Syria	12	11.5	31	242	26	1,286	10	64	55	2,115	55	99	44	27	32	85	98	43/76	57
United Arab Emir.	24	6.7	6	1,087	99	97	32	30	11	16,308	31	358	22	19	37	83	83	63/70	43
Yemen, Arab Rep.	25	6.6	71	42	52	482	42	107	93	635	78	35	108	68	97	62	138	3/27	105
Yemen, People's Dem. Rep.	5	20.0	54	83	54	454	24	108	102	414	89	25	92	47	106	51	117	25/59	101
South Asia		4.2		12		42,537				295		10		58		56		28/54	
Afghanista		•••		•••		•••		103		•••		•••	133	196	134	17	134	8/39	100
Bangladesh	105	1.7	125	3	20	1,774	90	130	130	164	127	3	122	112	123	37	119	22/43	123
India	54	3.9	93	12	3	31,283	45	110	114	314	107	11	94	51	93	64	113	29/57	102
Nepal	114	1.2	132	2	78	215	121	134	134	154	125	4	98	59	104	54	129	12/39	114
Pakistan	22	7.9	83	23	6	8,758	23	123	116	294	114	7	121	102	128	29	124	19/40	122
Sri Lanka	66	3.1	93	12	49	507	69	82	103	402	102	15	63	32	32	85	56	83/91	63
Far East		1.8		34		61,831				55,027		90		28		79		65/85	
Brunei	17	8.9	4	1,181	124	21	40	34	18	13,257	21	552	•••	•••	98	•••	70	69/85	46
Burma	94	1.9	121	5	38	739	91	110	118	258	120	5	108	68	98	60	76	66/89	101
Cambodia		•••		•••		•••		105	131	157		•••	96	58	120	40	79	65/85	74
China	49	4.4	92	13	1	47,027	36	91	117	285	112	8	44	27	47	80	88	56/82	73
Indonesia	89	2.1	108	8	10	3,617	69	98	107	378	104	13	41	26	44	81	79	65/83	67
■ Japan	120	1.0	37	198	27	1,236	58	7	5	19,582	9	979	35	22	9	93	4	99/99	14
Korea, North	15	10.0	48	117	15	2,139	12	69	72	1,169		•••		•••		•••		•••/•••	•••
Korea, South	39	4.8	42	145	16	2,009	17	51	46	3,049	50	120	83	41	28	86	40	88/96	50
Laos		•••		•••		•••		119	135	142	133	1	74	35	92	65	66	76/92	91
Malaysia	45	4.5	55	82	39	729	35	57	58	1,832	47	126	54	30	51	79	76	66/81	57
Mongolia	14	10.9	53	85	77	220	40	62	89	779		•••	44	27	19	89	39	90/95	34
Philippines	98	1.8	97	11	34	1,035	82	85	94	589	105	12	81	40	32	85	52	85/86	68
Singapore	34	5.1	23	405	91	134	42	39	29	7,929	30	400	58	31	64	75	61	79/93	53
Taiwan	30	5.4	32	241	30	1,058	15	44	43	4,502	44	162		•••		•••	49	86/96	47
Thailand	60	3.5	79	31	17	1,867	49	80	82	888	83	32	68	33	98	60	40	88/94	72
Vietnam		•••		•••		•••		97	120	231		•••	85	43	88	68	62	78/90	78
Oceania		2.7		238		589				8,974		482		19		87		90/92	
■ Australia	77	2.7	27	299	57	441	54	14	22	10,955	20	577	6	14	1	100	19	98/98	12
Fiji	84	2.3	74	36	126	16	105	54	64	1,565	55	99	44	27	9	93	58	81/90	42
■ New Zealand	78	2.4	33	239	106	79	79	18	24	10,058	19	596	27	20	7	94	19	98/98	18
Papua New Guinea	110	1.4	97	11	115	53	120	100	88	794	75	40	114	73	119	41	104	35/55	103

HEALTH   ENVIRONMENT

Public Expenditures per Capita Rank	US$	Population per Physician Rank	No.	Infant Mortality[7] Rank	Rate	Life Expectancy[8] Rank	Years	Health Average Rank[8]	Total Fertility Rate Rank	Rate per Woman[9]	Deforestation Rank	1000 Hectares[10]	Energy Consumption Rank	Kilos per Capita[11]	CO₂ Emissions Rank	Million Metric Tons[12]	Greenhouse Gas Emissions Rank	Million Metric Tons[13]	Environment Average Rank[14]	
	680		**520**		**18**		**74**			**1.9**				**3,411**		**100.9**		**96.9**		**Other Europe**
63	27	36	684	60	40	36	72	48	49	3.0		...	88	1,180	68	2.7	26	1.5	55	Albania
13	880	28	516	18	10	25	74	21	2	1.5		...	111	3,465	100	14.8	90	17.0	81	■ Austria
7	1,055	21	449	3	6	9	76	10	11	1.7		...	130	5,573	98	14.6	80	13.0	93	■ Finland
20	526	39	723	13	9	25	74	24	40	2.5		...	104	2,455	85	7.7	76	9.2	84	■ Ireland
34	173	37	690	23	11	30	73	31	26	1.9		...	93	1,504	29	0.4	4	0.2	15	Malta
1	1,582	10	371	3	6	2	77	4	11	1.7		...	132	6,527	103	15.8	83	14.0	94	■ Sweden
4	1,373	34	654	5	7	2	77	11	7	1.6		...	117	4,129	92	10.9	87	16.0	81	■ Switzerland
37	140	30	542	47	25	36	72	38	30	2.0		...	101	2,114	113	34.1	101	26.0	104	Yugoslavia
																				ASIA
	42		**1,196**		**72**		**63**			**5.6**		**20**		**1,115**		**180.2**		**174.6**		**Middle East**
26	239	46	844	49	26	41	71	41	66	4.1		...	138	11,377	75	4.4	36	2.3	90	Bahrain
43	106	42	746	25	12	9	76	30	37	2.3		...	94	1,599	52	1.1	14	0.5	32	Cyprus
94	7	44	804	95	85	84	61	79	74	4.7		...	69	574	107	20.5	90	17.0	100	Egypt
63	27	86	3,036	78	65	78	63	76	86	5.6	24	20	82	876	117	39.7	108	33.0	95	Iran
75	15	75	1,795	81	69	71	64	76	108	6.4		...	72	732	95	13.1	77	9.3	108	Iraq
36	151	20	446	25	12	15	75	24	47	2.9		...	98	1,968	87	8.1	77	9.3	87	■ Israel
58	33	61	1,223	64	44	64	66	62	133	7.1		...	73	745	68	2.7	21	1.2	77	Jordan
21	388	35	664	38	19	30	73	31	74	4.7		...	122	4,740	89	9.1	108	38.0	130	Kuwait
	...	50	921	60	40	61	67	43	55	3.4		...	81	845	65	2.3	20	1.0	48	Lebanon
40	123	56	1,076	104	100	97	55	74	136	7.2		...	102	2,174	80	5.9	59	4.7	121	Oman
	...	27	502	54	31	55	69	34	86	5.6		...	139	17,071	70	3.1	45	2.9	100	Qatar
28	212	38	698	84	71	78	63	57	136	7.2		...	113	3,567	119	46.2	114	42.0	137	Saudi Arabia
88	9	65	1,306	69	48	67	65	72	123	6.7		...	83	901	84	7.6	80	3.7	103	Syria
35	163	43	765	49	26	41	71	42	74	4.7		...	127	5,062	97	14.0	73	8.4	116	United Arab Emir.
99	6	92	5,622	118	118	113	51	106	129	7.0		...	33	112	46	0.9	15	0.6	50	Yemen, Arab Rep.
84	10	89	3,782	121	120	113	51	102	123	6.7		...	71	713	60	1.5	16	0.7	68	Yemen, People's Dem. Rep.
	2		**2,836**		**104**		**57**			**4.7**		**1,659**		**184**		**173.3**		**278.3**		**South Asia**
	...	93	5,884	142	172	142	40	94	127	6.9		...	31	92	52	1.1	31	1.8	60	Afghanistan
125	1	96	6,587	120	119	113	51	114	83	5.5	17	8	17	47	72	3.4	22	22.0	52	Bangladesh
109	3	82	2,621	103	99	91	58	96	68	4.3	77	1,500	46	207	133	152.9	134	230.0	115	India
125	1	129	20,612	126	128	113	51	123	95	5.9	46	84	7	23	15	0.2	67	6.8	27	Nepal
125	1	80	2,266	112	109	97	55	104	108	6.4	18	9	43	192	98	14.6	84	15.0	75	Pakistan
94	7	101	7,202	57	33	48	70	75	42	2.6	38	58	39	158	52	1.1	43	2.7	21	Sri Lanka
	80		**1,721**		**41**		**68**			**2.6**		**2,725**		**729**		**1,023.8**		**1,089.1**		**Far East**
43	106	64	1,268	25	12	25	74	39		...		...	134	7,195	44	0.8		...	...	Brunei
115	2	88	3,534	83	70	88	60	94	64	4.0	74	677	27	73	60	1.5	125	77.0	74	Burma
	...	120	14,775	127	130	123	48	93	74	4.7	28	30	22	59	4	0.1	61	5.1	14	Cambodia
104	4	73	1,670	55	32	55	69	72	38	2.4		...	68	573	137	595.2	135	380.0	122	China
115	2	107	8,009	93	82	91	58	102	54	3.3	76	920	47	215	114	34.6	130	140.0	97	Indonesia
11	987	33	637	1	5	1	78	12	11	1.7		...	109	3,237	136	251.0	133	220.0	127	■ Japan
78	12		...	49	26	55	69	61	59	3.6		...	100	2,077	118	40.3	94	20.0	116	Korea, North
80	11	62	1,257	47	25	55	69	61	30	2.0		...	91	1,456	121	47.9	105	29.0	105	Korea, South
	...	94	6,298	113	110	123	48	110	88	5.7	56	130	11	37	4	0.1	108	38.0	42	Laos
62	28	83	2,744	45	24	48	70	60	57	3.5	65	255	77	787	93	11.4	101	26.0	89	Malaysia
80	11	13	390	65	45	71	64	57	82	5.4		...	87	1,174	67	2.5	34	1.9	68	Mongolia
104	4	97	6,666	65	45	71	64	84	68	4.3	58	143	51	243	91	9.9	113	40.0	83	Philippines
45	99	49	902	13	9	30	73	34	7	1.6		...	119	4,426	86	7.9	69	7.1	76	Singapore
41	113	52	1,019	38	19	30	73	40	20	1.8		...		...		...		...	...	Taiwan
84	10	91	5,612	59	39	71	64	76	40	2.5	69	397	57	332	101	15.6	121	67.0	88	Thailand
	...	87	3,109	70	55	71	64	76	66	4.1	61	173	30	91	77	5.1	108	38.0	72	Vietnam
	504		**601**		**25**		**72**			**2.5**		**25**		**1,737**		**71.3**		**74.7**		**Oceania**
19	607	25	487	8	8	9	76	15	20	1.8		...	123	4,792	124	64.7	120	63.0	124	■ Australia
53	38	76	1,986	49	26	48	70	57	52	3.2	5	2	65	510	15	0.2	4	0.2	5	Fiji
17	634	32	560	23	11	15	75	22	26	1.9		...	118	4,259	79	5.8	79	10.0	78	■ New Zealand
67	24	117	13,225	71	59	101	54	89	88	5.7	27	23	49	224	35	0.6	26	1.5	24	Papua New Guinea

	MILITARY								GNP		EDUCATION								
	Public Expenditures				Equivalent Years of Income[1]		Military Burden[2]	Economic-Social Standing[3]	per Capita		Public Expenditures per Capita		School-Age Population per Teacher[4]		School-Age Population in School[4]		Literacy Rate[5]		Education[6]
	Rank	% of GNP	Rank	per Capita	Rank	1,000 Years	Average Rank	Average Rank	Rank	US$	Rank	US$	Rank	No.	Rank	%	F Rank	F/M %	Average Rank
AFRICA		4.4		27		20,000				620		36		65		50		37/57	
Sub-Sahara Africa		4.2		13		16,094				322		13		80		46		34/54	
• Other Africa		4.6		96		3,906				2,085		150		34		69		53/68	
• Algeria	94	1.9	62	52	56	446	77	66	48	2,682	36	268	63	32	67	74	103	37/63	67
Angola	5	20.0	34	221	19	1,845	7	106	76	1,106	81	33	117	79	109	49	107	32/49	104
Benin	98	1.8	110	7	106	79	117	120	104	397	95	20	118	80	116	42	127	16/37	114
Botswana	28	6.0	56	71	110	69	64	75	70	1,182	54	109	79	38	47	80	69	70/73	62
Burkina Faso	69	3.0	117	6	72	249	95	138	125	203	119	6	137	274	132	19	135	6/21	131
Burundi	72	2.9	117	6	87	143	102	129	123	222	114	7	131	181	127	32	116	26/43	122
Cameroon	94	1.9	84	22	81	199	95	95	73	1,166	83	32	108	68	89	67	95	45/68	94
Cen. African Rep.	98	1.8	110	7	117	48	121	121	105	391	95	20	127	148	120	40	113	29/53	114
Chad	38	4.9	110	7	71	257	80	140	137	133	127	3	136	222	128	29	131	11/40	131
Congo	45	4.5	65	50	103	83	77	86	75	1,115	65	60		•••		•••	89	55/71	77
Equatorial Guinea		•••		•••		•••	•••	93	111	329		•••	113	72	72	73		•••/•••	93
Ethiopia	18	8.8	97	11	9	3,849	26	142	139	123	120	5	128	167	128	29	137	5/11	128
Gabon	42	4.6	44	132	116	49	65	67	47	2,843	39	202	87	44	12	92	90	53/70	57
Gambia	15	10.0	88	20	106	79	73	131	127	200	114	7	105	66	116	42	128	15/36	116
Ghana	124	0.9	125	3	93	126	128	109	108	360	105	12	78	37	103	55	98	43/64	96
Guinea	69	3.0	105	9	82	191	94	132	115	311	111	9	130	180	132	19	126	17/40	125
Ivory Coast	114	1.2	97	11	89	139	111	102	83	847	72	51	111	69	114	45	108	31/53	101
Kenya	66	3.1	97	11	44	684	69	103	110	346	89	25	89	45	72	73	93	49/70	86
Lesotho	72	2.9	93	12	119	46	105	101	101	423	98	18	101	62	56	78	55	84/62	78
Liberia	78	2.4	97	11	113	56	107	112	100	458	98	18	116	78	128	29	118	23/47	115
• Libya	10	12.4	8	724	49	507	8	43	34	5,831	21	552	13	17	6	96	92	50/81	33
Madagascar	94	1.9	125	3	80	208	111	122	128	177	120	5	100	61	102	57	85	62/74	102
Malawi	98	1.8	125	3	90	137	116	135	133	156	120	5	125	126	110	48	108	31/52	116
Mali	62	3.3	110	7	67	280	87	137	124	218	114	7	133	196	136	15	131	11/23	129
Mauritania	42	4.6	85	21	102	86	82	117	99	466	88	27	122	112	125	35		•••/•••	112
Mauritius	134	0.2	124	4	133	2	134	59	62	1,638	67	58	44	27	56	78	64	77/89	58
• Morocco	35	5.0	78	34	28	1,167	36	99	91	686	77	39	87	44	105	52	119	22/45	97
Mozambique	21	8.0	110	7	29	1,163	51	139	140	87	127	3	129	179	126	34	119	22/55	125
Namibia		•••		•••		•••	•••	90	78	1,056	83	32	91	46	79	71	68	71/74	80
Niger	127	0.8	125	3	114	54	132	133	113	321	109	10	135	216	134	17	133	9/19	128
Nigeria	127	0.8	132	2	36	786	110	126	122	229	127	3	119	84	106	51	108	31/54	115
Rwanda	98	1.8	117	6	95	115	115	124	112	328	107	11	126	127	115	43	106	33/61	114
Senegal	85	2.2	90	14	86	149	98	116	92	644	87	29	124	114	122	38	124	19/37	114
Sierra Leone	127	0.8	134	1	121	31	133	136	129	174	132	2	102	63	113	46	122	21/38	117
Somalia	78	2.4	125	3	84	164	107	141	136	141	133	1	132	184	137	10	135	6/18	134
• South Africa	51	4.2	52	100	24	1,374	28	68	53	2,397	52	115	70	34	75	72	52	85/85	62
Sudan	28	6.0	76	35	23	1,381	28	118	95	579	92	24	120	89	124	36	123	20/44	115
Swaziland	111	1.3	97	11	129	9	125	87	85	829	72	51	74	35	39	82	76	66/70	65
Tanzania	32	5.3	110	7	25	1,309	56	125	138	131	120	5	115	77	116	42	40	88/93	98
Togo	58	3.6	90	14	97	114	89	113	106	381	89	25	112	71	95	63	115	28/54	103
• Tunisia	30	5.4	57	65	59	412	42	76	69	1,196	64	65	74	35	67	74	100	41/68	76
Uganda	78	2.4	121	5	60	398	95	128	126	202	127	3	105	66	112	47	95	45/70	110
Zaire	107	1.6	125	3	48	523	103	127	131	157	125	4	105	66	110	48	95	45/79	109
Zambia	58	3.6	108	8	70	274	85	114	121	230	112	8	102	63	86	69	74	67/84	94
Zimbabwe	20	8.1	70	44	41	720	33	83	98	542	68	57	79	38	12	92	74	67/82	58

■ Developed country   • Other Africa   — none or negligible   ••• not available

General Note   Averages (regional and other) represent only the countries for which data are reported. Summary measures are weighted by total population, female population, or births, as appropriate.
 1. Represents annual military expenditures per country divided by per capita GNP.
 2. Average of ranks for the three indicators of military expenditures shown.
 3. Average of ranks for: GNP per capita, education, and health.
 4. Ages 6–17; refers to general education only.
 5. Percent of adults (over 15), female and male, able to read and write; rank reflects female literacy only.
 6. Average of ranks for the four indicators of education shown.
 7. Deaths under 1 year of age per 1,000 live births.
 8. Average of ranks for the four indicators of health shown.
 9. Represents number of children who would be born per woman through her child-bearing years (usually 15–49) if she were to have children at prevailing age-specific rates.
10. Average annual area of forest lands permanently cleared for agriculture or settlements in the 1980's.
11. Consumption of commercial forms of energy, oil, natural gas, solid fuels, and primary electricity, all converted into oil equivalents.
12. Carbon dioxide emissions from fossil fuels and cement manufacture.
13. Current annual additions to the atmosphere of the three major greenhouse gases, carbon dioxide, methane, and chlorofluorocarbons, expressed in metric tons of carbon.
14. Average of ranks for the five environmental indicators shown. Since this selection is experimental and tentative, it is not included in "economic-social standing."

RANK shows the standing of the country among those in the table. The rank order number is repeated if more than one country has the same figure.

HEALTH   ENVIRONMENT

Public Expenditures per Capita		Population per Physician		Infant Mortality[7]		Life Expectancy[8]		Health	Total Fertility Rate		Deforestation		Energy Consumption		CO2 Emissions		Greenhouse Gas Emissions		Environment	
Rank	US$	Rank	No.	Rank	Rate	Rank	Years	Average Rank[8]	Rank	Rate per Woman[9]	Rank	1000 Hectares[10]	Rank	Kilos per Capita[11]	Rank	Million Metric Tons[12]	Rank	Million Metric Tons[13]	Average Rank[14]	
	7		6,432		109		52			6.4		3,764		321		150.1		321.8		**AFRICA**
	3		12,094		114		50			6.7		3,706		103		37.3		239.0		Sub-Sahara Africa
	26		1,951		75		61			5.0		58		1,382		112.8		82.8		• Other Africa
56	35	79	2,265	89	74	78	63	76	98	6.0	32	40	84	1,036	106	19.3	99	25.0	96	• Algeria
80	11	126	18,452	140	160	137	44	121	108	6.4	51	94	45	202	56	1.2	51	3.4	63	Angola
109	3	125	16,573	116	115	126	47	119	129	7.0	39	67	16	46	4	0.1	23	1.3	20	Benin
50	45	103	7,231	80	67	90	59	81	106	6.3	24	20	61	426	29	0.4	19	0.9	31	Botswana
115	2	139	55,367	133	138	126	47	128	116	6.5	43	80	2	18	4	0.1	37	2.4	19	Burkina Faso
115	2	130	22,736	115	112	121	49	120	106	6.3	3	1	4	20	1	<0.1	1	0.1	1	Burundi
84	10	123	15,297	99	94	109	52	104	91	5.8	62	190	37	149	62	1.6	87	16.0	71	Cameroon
102	5	113	11,263	129	132	131	46	119	95	5.9	37	55	9	31	4	0.1	31	1.8	9	Cen. African Rep.
125	1	134	37,629	129	132	131	46	130	95	5.9	43	80	2	18	4	0.1	37	2.4	12	Chad
69	23	104	7,654	88	73	118	50	95	98	6.0	26	22	53	251	31	0.5	29	1.6	30	Congo
...	...	...	...	124	127	131	46	62	88	5.7	9	3	22	59	1	<0.1	1	0.1	3	Equatorial Guinea
115	2	140	73,083	138	154	140	42	133	104	6.2	48	88	6	22	40	0.7	71	7.8	43	Ethiopia
50	45	85	2,939	103	103	109	52	88	81	5.0	23	15	85	1,134	57	1.4	25	1.4	46	Gabon
109	3	114	11,271	136	150	138	43	124	108	6.4	12	5	24	68	1	<0.1	4	0.2	6	Gambia
104	4	102	7,213	98	90	101	54	101	108	6.4	42	72	35	127	44	0.8	65	6.3	57	Ghana
109	3	138	53,167	135	147	138	43	130	104	6.2	47	86	18	49	24	0.3	60	4.8	33	Guinea
76	14	127	18,570	101	96	109	52	103	139	7.4	72	510	40	166	57	1.4	116	47.0	98	Ivory Coast
94	7	110	9,627	85	72	91	58	95	140	8.1	31	39	32	97	57	1.4	47	3.1	62	Kenya
91	8	118	13,567	104	100	95	56	102	91	5.8		...	1	10		...		...	...	Lesotho
91	8	111	9,671	96	87	101	54	100	116	6.5	33	46	42	170	15	0.2	54	4.0	36	Liberia
33	187	41	729	91	80	84	61	62	126	6.8		...	106	2,679	82	7.2	57	4.5	116	• Libya
104	4	109	9,072	121	120	101	54	109	121	6.6	60	156	12	38	15	0.2	80	13.0	53	Madagascar
109	3	137	44,865	134	145	131	46	128	129	7.0	59	150	13	41	4	0.1	70	7.3	47	Malawi
115	2	131	25,967	141	169	126	47	128	123	6.7	29	36	5	21	4	0.1	35	2.1	17	Mali
88	9	115	12,427	124	127	131	46	115	116	6.5	20	13	34	113	46	0.9	17	0.8	29	Mauritania
60	28	67	1,400	43	23	61	67	58	26	1.9	1	<1	60	374	24	0.3	4	0.2	1	Mauritius
94	7	90	5,297	93	82	84	61	90	79	4.8	20	13	51	243	78	5.5	49	3.3	49	• Morocco
115	2	136	43,803	136	150	126	47	128	108	6.4	53	120	29	86	24	0.3	52	3.6	41	Mozambique
99	6	95	6,315	108	105	95	56	99	101	6.1		...		...		...		...	...	Namibia
115	2	135	38,171	132	135	136	45	130	133	7.1	40	67	15	45	15	0.2	26	1.5	26	Niger
134	<1	100	7,177	108	105	113	51	114	129	7.0	70	400	36	139	101	15.6	118	53.0	113	Nigeria
115	2	133	34,363	123	122	121	49	123	141	8.3	12	5	13	41	4	0.1	9	0.3	11	Rwanda
94	7	121	15,091	127	130	123	48	116	108	6.4	34	50	38	155	35	0.6	47	3.1	39	Senegal
125	1	119	14,256	138	154	141	41	131	116	6.5	16	6	28	77	15	0.2	17	0.8	16	Sierra Leone
134	<1	122	15,256	129	132	126	47	128	121	6.6	22	14	24	68	24	0.3	37	2.4	25	Somalia
76	14	69	1,448	85	72	88	60	80	71	4.5	71	...	105	2,473	126	77.6	116	47.0	134	• South Africa
125	1	112	10,056	111	108	118	50	117	108	6.4	71	504	21	58	46	0.9	84	15.0	66	Sudan
71	19	106	7,911	118	118	97	55	98	116	6.5	1	<1	56	291	4	0.1	1	0.1	10	Swaziland
125	1	128	20,407	100	106	105	53	115	133	7.1	56	130	10	34	35	0.6	58	4.6	56	Tanzania
99	6	124	15,740	100	95	105	53	107	101	6.1	19	12	20	54	4	0.1	11	0.4	8	Togo
66	26	77	2,061	72	60	67	65	71	64	4.0	12	5	64	496	71	3.3	46	3.0	35	• Tunisia
125	1	132	26,348	106	103	118	50	120	127	6.9	34	50	8	25	15	0.2	31	1.8	22	Uganda
125	1	116	13,079	102	98	109	52	113	101	6.1	68	370	26	72	51	1.0	87	16.0	67	Zaire
104	4	108	8,403	91	80	105	53	102	136	7.2	41	70	59	365	40	0.7	41	2.5	65	Zambia
70	20	98	6,801	85	72	91	58	86	91	5.8	43	80	66	522	74	4.2	64	5.9	70	Zimbabwe

NOTES ON DATA

The notes following provide a brief background on definitions and sources, and are intended to alert the general reader to some of the measurement problems in an international compilation of this kind. Readers wishing to use the detailed figures for analytical purposes are urged to consult the original sources, which more adequately convey the scope and qualifications of the data.

Specific queries may be addressed to the author (Box 25140, Washington, D.C. 20007). Professional comments and suggestions are welcome at all times, and particularly from national statistical services which could add to the accuracy of the reporting.

Revisions—In compiling this 14th edition of *World Military and Social Expenditures,* all statistics were reviewed and corrected to include the most recent data available for the 142 countries that are covered. Because of revisions by original sources and the changes in sources that are sometimes necessary, the national data in Tables II and III cannot be used as a time series, or to judge trends.

Time frame—Although the statistical tables were largely prepared in 1990, the latest year for which adequate world-wide coverage was possible for many of the social statistics was 1987, and for some it was 1980 or 1985. Social data tend to lag behind military. Projections were therefore necessary for some of the social statistics, while military, population, and GNP data were generally available through 1988.

Qualifications of the data—In the post-war period there has been a major leap forward in the availability and reliability of data for international comparisons. Nevertheless, any world compendium of this sort inevitably represents subjective judgments in selecting and presenting statistics, and includes data that are uneven in quality. Numerous factors affect comparability and suggest caution in making comparisons between countries. For example:

1. Some statistical systems, especially in developing nations, are in the early stages of development; beyond urban areas coverage may be nonexistent or extremely sparse.

2. The practice of limited disclosure of statistics continues particularly in countries under communist governments. In these cases the range of error in estimates made by foreign experts is unknown and may be wide. Most of the figures shown for Albania, China, Cuba, Laos, Mongolia, North Korea, Vietnam, and the Warsaw Pact countries are subject to considerable uncertainty and must be regarded as very rough approximations.

3. Hostilities in Afghanistan, Cambodia and Lebanon have restricted the flow of information from those countries. Where estimates are shown, they are rough benchmark data, largely based on earlier years.

4. Variations in definitions and concepts may significantly affect comparability. These occur even under the most advanced reporting systems and apply to centrally-planned as well as to other systems.

5. Per capita figures based on national totals reveal nothing of the pattern of distribution in incomes and welfare within countries. Differences within nations in those patterns may mean significant disparities in the level of living of the average citizen which are not apparent in gross indicators.

Gross National Product

Gross National Product is the economy's total output of goods and services, valued at current market prices paid by the ultimate consumer.

GNP, as stated above, is the most comprehensive measure of the national economy, but it does not cover some important areas of economic activity. Household services and that part of the product which is outside the market are not included in the GNP. For this reason, it is likely to be more representative, as a measure of overall product, for developed economies than for developing. The difference in coverage does not invalidate comparisons between the two groups of countries, but it may tend to exaggerate the contrast between them.

The GNP figures are drawn largely from the data fund of the World Bank. For non-communist countries, the Bank's calculations in national currencies are converted to dollars using 1987 exchange rates. The GNP estimate for the USSR is from the CIA *Handbook for Economic Statistics,* adjusted to a 1987 base. For the countries of Eastern Europe, GNP data are from the Research Project on

National Income in East Central Europe, by Thad Alton *et al.* Estimates for other communist countries represent a continuation of the series previously prepared by Dr. Herbert Block for the US State Department.

Military

National military expenditures are current and capital expenditures to meet the needs of the armed forces. They usually include military assistance to foreign countries and the military components of nuclear, space, and research and development programs.

IMF reporting, which is the source used for military expenditures for most countries in this publication, excludes expenditures for pensions and war veterans affairs, and includes civil defense and foreign military aid. On the other hand, NATO reporting (used here for NATO countries) includes pensions, and also the cost of paramilitary forces when equipped for military operations.

IISS, *The Military Balance,* the *SIPRI Yearbook,* and national and regional publications which report on military spending are also consulted for this compilation.

Because of differences in national accounting practices, and uncertainties with respect to such classified outlays as national intelligence, it is especially difficult to achieve general uniformity in this budget category. Understatement of military outlays is probably more common than overstatement. (See especially Nicole Ball, *Third World Security Expenditures,* Stockholm) There are also substantial social costs which are extra-budgetary, including manpower underpriced because of conscription, the tax exemptions accorded military properties, and some privately-financed R&D. Because extra-budgetary costs are not reflected in official budgets, military expenditures also tend to understate the burden on the economy.

In Warsaw Pact and other communist countries, the scope of the accounting for military programs is not clear and estimates are necessarily highly speculative. In China and the USSR, defense budgets are a single line item in the central government budget, undefined as to scope.

Armed forces represent manpower in the regular active-duty forces, including conscripts. Paramilitary forces and reservists are not included.

The manpower figures in the tables cover regular forces only, on the premise that these provide the most consistent basis for international comparison, and also are covered by military budgets. Paramilitary forces (armed border guards and gendarmerie) vary considerably in their potential for prompt and efficient military action, as do reservists, who serve for a short period in the year. (The addition of paramilitary and reservist forces would raise the world total of men under arms to about 100 million.)

In individual countries, the significance of the size of the force will depend on their equipment, training, technical proficiency, and morale, and also (as in the US) on the use made of civilians in functions that are performed by the military in other countries. Some categories of regular forces may be included in paramilitary or (as in the US recently), transferred to active reserves. Some countries have universal, automatic draft for relatively short periods; others, like the US, depend on volunteers, who serve on a career basis and generally for longer periods.

IISS, the recognized international authority on force levels, also publishes data on paramilitary forces, people's milita, and reservists.

Arms trade represents the transfer to governments of conventional military equipment and of commodities considered primarily military in nature. Nuclear materials are excluded.

The trade estimates are from ACDA, as published in dollars. While the ACDA coverage is reported to conform to the definition above, there is no information given on the method of valuing equipment or commodities. ACDA receives the data already expressed in current dollars. It should also be noted that services, such as construction, training, and technical support, are included for all countries except the US.

The data include weapons, military aircraft and ships, ammunition, uniforms, and exclude foodstuffs, medical equipment, and other items with alternative civilian uses. They are trade figures, and therefore do not cover orders or agreements which may result in future transfers. They also omit other significant routes for arms shipments, such as commercial black market trade, official but covert arms supply, and licensed coproduction abroad. These and other unrecorded channels would significantly raise estimates of the international arms trade.

Military Control and Repression

The criteria used for establishing the list of military-controlled governments, and the classifications of official use of violence, are shown below *map 2,* page 18.

The principal sources of information were:
for "military-controlled governments": *Europa Yearbook, World Factbook, Statesman's Yearbook, International Yearbook, Deadline Data on World Affairs, South, Africa Report,* and *World Press Review.*

for "official violence": US Department of State *Country Reports on Human Rights Practices,* and publications of Amnesty International and of Human Rights Watch (including Africa Watch, Americas Watch, Asia Watch, Helsinki Watch, and Middle East Watch).

Since the political role of the military and governments' use of these extreme forms of repression vary both in degree and in the evidence available, the general classifications used here were necessarily a matter of subjective judgment in a number of cases, and may well be open to dispute.

Wars and Deaths

Wars and estimated deaths are from records maintained by William Eckhardt, Research Director, Lentz Peace Research Laboratory, St. Louis, Missouri. These records, which were updated through December 1990, are constantly revised as new information is obtained.

Because we do not have space to print all the references, a photocopy of Eckhardt's sources for wars and deaths in wars is available on request to World Priorities.

Information on deaths associated with wars is incomplete and Eckhardt emphasizes that all estimates must be used with caution. No central official records are kept. Civilian deaths are less reliable than battle deaths and are often unavailable. War-related famine was a major cause of high death rates in conflicts in Nigeria, Bangladesh, Cambodia, and southern Africa.

Nuclear

Nuclear reactors—The world's inventory of nuclear reactors, shown on the map pages 14–15, is from *Nuclear News, Nuclear Engineering International,* the International Atomic Energy Agency, and for the US, the US Department of Energy. Power reactors are operable as of December 31, 1988, or expected to operate by 1995. Research reactors are from IAEA and US Department of Energy.

Nuclear Weapons—The number of nuclear weapons in the stockpiles of the superpowers *(chart 8)* and the total held by the six nuclear powers are calculated by the Nuclear Weapons Data Project of the NRDC.

The energy yield of nuclear stockpiles in early 1991 is roughly estimated by the NRDC at 15,000–16,000 megatons in TNT equivalent. Estimates of the TNT equivalent of all munitions expended in prior wars are by Arthur H. Westing in *Bulletin of Peace Proposals,* No. 1, 1985.

Map 1, the ninth edition of The Nuclear World, updates the locations of reactors and the infrastructure supporting nuclear weapons. The classifications of countries are, with some deviations, essentially based on the research of Leonard Spector, published in five volumes by the Carnegie Endowment. In addition to 6 "nuclear powers," the map shows 3 states with "nuclear weapons capability" (states judged to have the essentials for A-bombs), 7 "emerging nuclear powers" (states with interest or facilities that might in the years ahead lead to bombs), and 7 states with nuclear weapons stationed on their soil.

NRDC and IPS nuclear studies have been major sources of information for weapons locations and test sites shown on the maps. Another source for test sites is UN's report of 12 September 1980. Some of these sites (e.g. the two in Australia) are no longer in use. Reprocessing facilities are from a report by Pacific Northwest Laboratory for the US Department of Energy, November 1984. Since this map has been built up over the years, please see earlier editions for other sources of data.

Education

Public education expenditures represent current and capital expenditures by governments for public education and subsidized private education for preschool through university levels.

UNESCO is the principal source of all data on education. Where necessary, other sources were used to supplement data for 1984, including national statistical journals and national accounts compiled by IMF and OECD.

In compiling information on public education expenditures, UNESCO attempts to cover such expenditures at local and intermediate levels of government as well as in the central government.

Since private education expenditures are not covered here, and nations vary greatly in the ratio of private to public spending, comparisons of total national expenditures may differ significantly from those for public only. In the US, for example, private funds cover over one-quarter of all education expenditures. In centrally planned economies, non-public funding is also significant, but it is likely to be a smaller proportion of the total.

Teachers and students are those in both public and private schools, through secondary or high school levels, not including pre-school, teacher training, vocational, and adult education.

The count of teachers includes those working part-time. Instructional personnel without teaching functions (e.g. supervisors and librarians) are excluded by UNESCO insofar as it is possible to do so. Enrollment includes all ages and therefore may exceed the population of the official school ages as defined by each country.

Literacy rates represent the proportion of the adult population (generally 15 years and over) who can, with understanding, both read and write a short, simple statement related to their everyday life.

Standardized tests for literacy focus on basic skills, the ability to read and write on a lower elementary school level. The concept of literacy is changing, however, particularly in industrialized countries, where there is increased awareness of the requirement for functional literacy, sometimes defined as the ability to read instructions necessary for a job or a license. By these standards, illiteracy is much more common than basic rates suggest.

Health Care

Public expenditures on health represent current and capital expenditures by governments for medical care and other health services.

They include national health insurance, public health, health expenditures under workmen's compensation, and in some countries, public expenditures for family planning, social welfare and social security. They do not include private health expenditures (and it should be noted that the ratio of private to public spending varies greatly among nations).

In some countries health expenditures by governments are understated because of incomplete reporting at intermediate and local levels of government. To the extent that they include outlays for health care for military personnel, however, they overstate the size of civilian programs and may represent some double counting.

In addition to variations in coverage, WHO has cautioned that differences in budgetary concepts and definitions of health seriously qualify comparisons among countries.

The major sources of data on expenditures are: IMF *Government Finance Statistics Yearbook* and OECD publications, for the 24 OECD countries.

Physicians refer to fully qualified doctors practicing in the country.

This is intended to be a count of doctors in active practice, teaching, or performing research within the country. National reporting, however, may reflect differences in definition, as well as in qualifications and training of physicians. Some countries include registered physicians who are inactive or who are practicing elsewhere. Some, including Italy and USSR, count dentists as physicians. Some report only physicians in government service. Despite these shortcomings, the national data on physicians are probably more reliable for inter-country comparisons than are expenditure figures.

Environment

For terms and references see column opposite. Sources of specific data in tables and charts are given below.

Carbon dioxide (CO_2) emissions resulting from fossil fuel consumption, cement production, and gas flaring are estimated by Oak Ridge National Laboratory, Tennessee, USA 37831. Projections of CO_2 to the year 2025 are from the *EPA Journal* of the US Environmental Protection Agency (EPA).

Energy consumption refers to commercial forms of primary energy (petroleum and natural gas liquids, natural gas, coal and lignite, and primary electricity). Data are from the UN *Energy Statistics Yearbook* and a World Bank print.

Forests (reforestation and deforestation) are from the World Resources Institute and World Bank, *Social Indicators of Development*.

Fuel economy data, in miles per gallon of gasoline are from EPA and, in goals for the year 2000, from the American Council for an Energy-Efficient Economy.

Gasoline prices and taxes are reported quarterly for the OECD countries by OECD in *Energy Prices and Taxes*.

Global warming and **greenhouse gas** emissions are from reports of the World Resources Institute and Worldwatch Institute.

Population data, including population projections, urban population, and births and deaths in relation to mother's education are from the UN Population Division.

Exchange Rates

In making international comparisons of value data, the choice of conversion rates so radically affects results that a statement on this point is owed the reader. There is at present no wholly adequate basis for converting national currencies world-wide into a common denominator such as US dollars.

Although statistical work on purchasing power parities is underway, under international sponsorship, the availability of parities for a large selection of countries is some distance in the future.

Like other compilations of international statistics, this report in most instances uses average exchange rates for conversion from national currencies to dollars. These rates measure currency relations in internationally-traded goods. They are by no means ideal for conversion of GNP and national budgets. They provide a rough basis for intercountry comparisons but may have the effect of understating the income of low-income countries.

Official exchange rates may also be subject to abrupt changes. As a result of these up and down shifts, a nation can seem to have moved into affluence, or depression, from one year to the next.

World Bank alternative conversion factors are used in those cases in which the Bank finds that the official exchange rate has diverged by a large margin from the effective rate used in foreign transactions.

Price Deflators

International comparisons with earlier years are affected by internal price trends as well as by changes in parities. To eliminate the impact of these fluctuations in the historical series, both national expenditures and GNP have been adjusted to the price base and exchange rates of 1987, using GNP deflators developed by the World Bank. Where World Bank deflators are not available, the US deflator is used.

Economic-Social Rank

Table III includes a single figure for each nation to summarize its rank among all nations in economic-social indicators. Three factors are combined: GNP per capita, education, and health. The method of averaging gives equal importance to each of the three elements. For education and health, this means that a summary rank, a simple average, is first obtained for the indicators shown under each category.

The ranking method makes it possible to combine a variety of indicators. Other combinations are, of course, possible, and will be further explored. In this case, the indicators chosen for education and health represent both input of national effort (e.g. public expenditures, teachers) and output (e.g. literacy, infant mortality). Input factors give credit for effort, which will determine social progress but may not yet show in slower-acting indicators of results. □

References on the Environment

Basic factual sources

Brower, Michael, *Cool Energy*, Union of Concerned Scientists, 1990.

Council for Environmental Quality, *Environmental Quality 1970–1990*, 1990.

Organization for Economic Cooperation and Development, (OECD), *OECD Environmental Data Compendium 1989* (bi-annual).

OECD, *State of the Environment*, 1991.

United Nations Environmental Programme (UNEP), *Environmental Data Report*, 1989–1990.

Union of Concerned Scientists, *Steering a New Course*, 1991.

United Nations Population Fund, *The State of the World Population 1990* (annual).

World Bank, *World Development Report 1990* (annual).

World Commission on Environment and Development, *Our Common Future*, 1987.

World Resources Institute, with UNEP and UNDP, *World Resources 1990–1991* (annual).

Worldwatch Institute, *State of the World 1991* (annual).

Terms

Acid rain: Deposition of droplets of sulfuric and nitric acid dissolved in rain and snow or of airborne particles of sulfate or nitrate salts.

Agroforestry: Fast-growing trees planted with food crops in order to produce sustained yields of food, forage, and wood.

BHC: Benzene hexachloride, a compound used as an insecticide.

Biological diversity: The complexity of an ecosystem, as measured by the number of plant and animal species and subspecies that system supports.

Biomass fuels: Also called "traditional fuels"—firewood, charcoal, animal dung, and crop wastes; important sources of energy in Third World.

Carcinogen: Cancer-producing substance.

CFCs: Chlorofluorocarbons, chlorine-containing pollutants which deplete atmospheric ozone and contribute to global warming.

Conservation: The protection and preservation of natural resources.

Desertification: Loss of land's productivity by erosion, salinization, waterlogging, and other forms of land degradation.

DDT: Synthetic water-soluble organic insecticide which is toxic; accumulates in ecosystem.

Energy efficiency: The rational and economical utilization of energy resources.

Fossil fuels: petroleum, natural gas, coal; the residues of the earth's store of fossil plants.

Global warming: See page 32.

Greenhouse gases: See page 32.

Intercropping: Growing two or more crops simultaneously on the same plot.

Ozone (ground): A form of oxygen, an irritating gas formed photochemically; a major agent in the formation of smog.

Ozone layer: See page 31.

PCBs: Polychlorinated biphenyls, heat-resistant chemicals used as coolants in electrical equipment; banned in US since 1977.

Renewable resources: Energy drawn from the vast, inexhaustible resources of sunlight, wind, river, oceans, and plants.

Salinization: The accumulation of salts in soil as surface water evaporates, often from over-irrigation; can degrade the land beyond the point it can support plant life.

Waterlogging: Damage to soil structure when poorly drained soil receives more water than it can absorb; affects land productivity and hinders plant growth.

Estimates of Soviet Military Expenditures:
A Critique

Franklyn D. Holzman

Debates over the level of Soviet military spending and of its ratio to GNP have been enriched over the past two years by the release of new and more reasonable estimates by the Soviet government and attacks on these estimates by Soviet critics. Since the information from Soviet sources remains incomplete or sketchily documented, US intelligence estimates will continue to be an important source of information for these key indicators of one of the largest economies in the world.

In the following review of the data available, the estimates of Soviet GNP by the Central Intelligence Agency (CIA) are accepted but, for reasons that are stated, that Agency's estimates of Soviet military expenditures and their relation to GNP are questioned. The critique does not provide a firm basis for an alternative, precise estimate of Soviet military expenditures but it may nevertheless serve as a useful reminder of the spongy ground on which the intense competition of the Cold War rested. As the record now stands, CIA's estimates in recent years appear to have overstated Soviet military expenditures by as much as $100 billion a year.

CIA Ruble Estimates

In the 1980's, CIA on two occasions revised upwards its estimates of Soviet military expenditures in relation to GNP, both indicators being expressed in rubles. Although later information, made public by the Agency itself, invalidated the reasons it had given for the upward adjustments, no equivalent downward corrections were made.

Over the decade, the sequence of changes in CIA estimates of the ratio of military expenditures to GNP was as follows:

■ In 1980, CIA revised its estimate of the ratio to GNP from 11–13 to 12–14 percent because, according to CIA, while military expenditures continued to rise at 4–5 percent a year, annual increases in GNP had declined to around 2 percent a year.

■ In 1983, CIA admitted that it had made an error in 1980, stating that after 1975, growth in military expenditures had also declined to 2 percent a year. Given this admission, one would have expected CIA to have revised the ratio back to 11–13 percent, since the reason for the increase to 12–14 percent was now admitted to have been in error. This was not done and no explanation was given for the failure to make the correction.

■ In 1986, following a wide-ranging price reform in the USSR, CIA re-based its estimates of Soviet defense spending from 1970 prices into the new 1982 prices. As a result, the estimated ratio to Soviet GNP took a leap upward from 12–14 to 15–17 percent. The reason for the revision, according to CIA, was that prices of weapons had increased much faster than prices of civilian goods between 1970 and 1982.

■ Subsequently it developed that this disparity in the price rises was guesswork. In a pamphlet published in November 1987, the Agency conceded that it had been unable to obtain any new 1982 weapons' prices; further, that there was reason to believe that weapons' prices had risen more slowly than prices of civilian goods. Despite these admissions, CIA's estimate of Soviet ratio to GNP was not reduced from its 15–17 percent level.

Given the data both for military spending and GNP upon which CIA bases its estimates, I contend that a corrected ratio of Soviet military expenditures to GNP should be 9–11 rather than 15–17 percent. The calculations for this conclusion are spelled out in the box opposite.

Two factors may be cited which strongly support this critique of the CIA estimates.

First, on May 30, 1989 (after my initial article on this subject had been sent to press), Chairman Gorbachev announced both a projected military expenditure of 77.3 billion rubles for 1989 and a ratio to GNP that he put at 9 percent. The difference between Gorbachev's 9 percent and my 10 percent (9–11 percent averaged as 10 percent) is due primarily to different concepts for estimating GNP used by the Soviets and CIA.

Second, in the Spring 1990 issue of *International Security*, CIA officially attacked the arguments presented above in a letter signed by James Steiner. In my opinion, expressed in a letter published along with Steiner's, CIA failed to explain why the errors which I had identified had not been corrected after new evidence had been obtained.

Re-estimating the Estimates

My calculations are as follows: a 1 percentage-point error was introduced in 1980 when CIA raised the ratio of military expenditures to GNP from 11–13 to 12–14 percent; and a 3 percentage-point error was introduced in 1986 when the military expenditure ratio was raised still further to 15–17 percent as a result of the alleged shift to 1982 prices. Actually, based on index number theory grounds, the shift from 1970 to 1982 prices should have resulted in a decline in the ratio. I assume that the decline should have been about 10 percent, i.e. from 11–13 percent to 10–12 percent because, according to CIA, the industry/GNP ratio fell from 36 to 33 percent, or by about 10 percent, as a result of the shift from 1970 to 1982 ruble prices.

A further 1 percentage-point adjustment, to 9–11 percent, is justified because CIA includes in Soviet military expenditures a number of civilian expenditures not included in US military expenditures such as: civil defense, civilian space, logging and road building.[1]

Franklyn D. Holzman, Professor Emeritus at Tufts University, and Fellow, Harvard Research Center, recently tied for first prize in the Firth International Ruble Convertibility Competion, to which over 650 economists and financial specialists from 17 countries submitted proposals for a convertible ruble. The USSR has not yet acted to make the ruble convertible.

Nor has CIA yet responded satisfactorily to the questions Professor Holzman raised in 1989 regarding the Agency's estimates of Soviet military expenditures. For the record, he summarizes his criticisms here.

CIA Dollar Estimates

Perhaps the best known estimates made by the CIA are its comparisons of Soviet and US military expenditures in dollars. These estimates provided an important rationale for the most expensive arms competition in history.

Possibly because these estimates had been subjected to strong methodological criticisms, their public dissemination ceased about a decade ago. Recently, however, estimates in chart form were released.[2] The trouble with the methodology of CIA's dollar estimates, as the Agency has often acknowledged, is that it exaggerates Soviet military expenditures relative to US military expenditures, even as a ruble comparison would exaggerate US military expenditures relative to Soviet.

A less-biased way of making such comparisons is to value and then compare the two nations' military expenditures in dollars and in rubles, finally taking an average (geometric mean) of the two comparisons. This is standard practice and is how the CIA makes most of its other US-Soviet economic comparisons, including GNP.[3].

In its most recent published dollar estimates, CIA states that ". . . the cumulative dollar value of Soviet defense activities has exceeded comparable U.S. defense outlays by more than 20 percent over the past 15 years [1972-1987]."[4] The chart published with the statement shows a trend in which, presumably, Soviet military expenditures exceeded those of the US by about 40 percent in the early years of the period but, due to the US buildup in the 1980's, the two nations' military expenditures are about equal in 1987 at almost $300 billion.

I have adjusted these figures for the exaggerations mentioned earlier with regard to the ruble estimates of Soviet military expenditures and also for the fact that the comparison is made in dollars rather than as an average of estimates in both dollars and rubles. The revised estimates, necessarily crude, nevertheless suggest that Soviet military expenditures not only did not exceed US military expenditures over the 1972-1987 period by more than 20 percent, as CIA claims, but may in fact have been somewhat less than US expenditures.

One might ask: why has the CIA engaged in these unprofessional practices in their estimates of Soviet military expenditures when most of their other work on the Soviet economy is characterized by high scholarly standards? Two possible explanations come to mind.

Because of the cold war, there have undoubtedly been pressures on CIA to bias upward, wherever possible, their estimates of Soviet military expenditures. It is much easier to get increased appropriations for our own military expenditures if it can be shown that Soviet military expenditures are high and growing rapidly.

Related to the above, CIA has been in competition with DIA (Defense Intelligence Agency, the Pentagon's research unit) which makes its own ruble estimates of Soviet military expenditures and ratios of military expenditures to GNP. Before 1985, DIA's figures were always higher than those of CIA. There is evidence of a struggle between the two Agencies in 1983-84 regarding the relative correctness of their estimates. One can conjecture that a compromise was reached, apparently favoring DIA.[5] The result has been that CIA's figures for Soviet military expenditures and ratios to GNP have recently been identical with those of DIA despite the fact that they are quite inconsistent with CIA's earlier estimates.

Unfortunately, lacking detailed public information on the dollar equivalents of the elements of Soviet military expenditures, or even a free market rate for the ruble, it has been impossible for outside specialists to develop a solid basis for dollar estimates. Using CIA's own (preliminary) estimate for 1988 of GNP at factor cost, which was 732 billion rubles in 1982 rubles, and CIA's implied military ruble/dollar ratio of about 1r=$2.5, Soviet military expenditures in 1988 would have been $165-201 billion at the 9-11 percent military expenditures ratio and $275-311 billion at the 15-17 percent ratio.

The chart presented by Swain (CIA)[3] suggests an estimate for 1987 of approximately $295 billion in 1986$US—or about $304 billion in 1987$US. This result compares with an estimate of $303 billion, or 12.7 percent of GNP, published by the US Arms Control and Disarmament Agency, and of $275 billion, or 11.4 percent of GNP, by this publication.

Estimates by Soviet Critics

Gorbachev broke with Soviet practice in 1989 by announcing military expenditures for 1989 of 77.3 billion rubles and a ratio to GNP of 9 percent that purport to be accurate and complete.[6] This ruble figure, while almost four times higher than previous official Soviet estimates (which the USSR now admits were incomplete), was nevertheless much lower than the estimates by individual Soviet "revisionist" economists and others that have appeared in the media with *glasnost'*. The critics' estimates of the military-to-GNP ratio have been in the 18-30 percent range. They have been higher than CIA's as a result of both lower estimates of Soviet GNP and higher estimates of Soviet military expenditures. While some of the points made by the Soviet economists bear consideration, in general their quantitative estimates lack substance and do not inspire confidence.[7]

One of the revisionists' major criticisms of CIA's GNP estimate is that it overestimates the quality of Soviet consumer products, hence the size of Soviet GNP. CIA has corrected its error in this regard. Moreover, CIA has also pointed out that this error has been offset by "downward errors" resulting from understatements of quality improvements in services and non-consumers' goods and of the value-added to GNP produced by the second economy.[8]

While individual Soviet critics have also suggested that Gorbachev's estimate of Soviet military expenditures is too low, to my knowledge no quantitative re-estimates have been made. This is undoubtedly due to the fact that there are almost no public data on which reliable re-estimates of military expenditures could be based. The views expressed have been mostly "guesstimates." The most convincing criticism made by revisionists is that military industries and military R&D have access to higher quality resources and personnel than the civilian sector and at no higher cost.[9] This point has often been made by western economists. If true, Soviet military expenditures would be understated. Unfortunately, the degree of understatement appears impossible to estimate.

The same Soviet economists have also argued that a substantial component of military expenditures is hidden in the budget under civilian categories. Related to this, another Soviet economist argues that military expenditures are understated in the budget as a result of subsidies which lower their prices to the Ministry of Defense.[10]

I have no way of evaluating these latter two arguments. These may (or may not) be identical since the alleged "subsidies" would probably be included in "other budget expenditure" categories.

●●●●●●

In summary, estimates of the size of the Soviet military expenditure effort and its percentage of Soviet GNP vary widely and all must be viewed with caution. The estimates of revisionists in the USSR are highest, followed closely by those of CIA; in fact, the CIA's estimate of 15-17 percent of GNP is very close to the revisionists' 18 percent "low end." Some may feel that CIA estimates are supported by the fact that revisionist estimates are in the same ballpark at the lower end. In fact, as noted above, CIA methodology, when properly corrected, leads to an estimate in the 9-11 percent range. There is, then, an extraordinary gap between an adjusted CIA measure and those of the revisionists. That a gap of this magnitude exists regarding the size of Soviet military expenditures indicates clearly the uncertainties attending estimates which were a critical factor in justifying our own enormous military budget.

See page 49 for references.

Superpower Productions

Act V
Bumble, bumble, toil and trouble

Weapons in Wonderland

*A short skit dedicated to the taxpayer who will
be pleased to see that the other twin is buying
less-kill-for-the-ruble/
less-bang-for-the-buck.*

The valiant US Patriot missile, made to kill aircraft, did its best against Iraqi Scud missiles, but its intercepting warheads also rained more explosives on densely populated cities below, increasing overall destruction.

In a demonstration flight for the US Defense Secretary, two Soviet Blackjack bombers—long touted by the Pentagon as one of the most threatening of the Soviet strategic systems—flew on a wing and a prayer, with only three of the four engines functioning.

The US Abrams tank, at $2.5 million each, is a formidable 60-ton monster, but it was not usable in the US invasion of Panama because it was too heavy to airlift and, in any case, would have collapsed Panama's bridges.

Shortages of replacement parts and frequent mechanical breakdowns have made many of the older submarines in the Soviet fleet more dangerous to their own crews than to their opponents.

Official US plans for storing nuclear weapons waste in molten glass had to be modified when environmentalists reminded officials that the chemical in the waste, secretly added 30 years ago, would explode if heated.

A close look at the Soviet early warning system—the alert against incoming attacks—gives comfort neither to its own citizens nor to potential enemies: false alarms are common.

The US air force, which several years ago lost a luxurious toilet seat to picky budget cutters, still has a yen to live like a king. Questioned about a $999 pair of pliers, the air force spokesman commented that the price charged was "fair and reasonable."

Undaunted by the unpopularity of the exploding TV set (*WMSE 89*), Soviet defense entrepreneurs continue their determined drive for a civilian market. One of the latest products is a heavyweight tank with the turret removed, to serve as a tracked fire engine.

Electronic features of the US Apache attack helicopter broke down so often when used in Panama that mechanics had to dry essential parts in kitchen ovens.

Another brainchild of the Soviet conversion to a market economy is a 120-ton construction crane mounted on a mobile missile launcher.

The US navy's cruise missile, the Tomahawk, is choosy about the terrain it flies over. As a naval official in the Gulf War explained, "If you fly it over flat desert, it doesn't work."

And still another clever Soviet adaptation to free enterprise: a commercial submarine with windows (no curtains) for sale to tourist companies.

The US development and production cost of the city-busting Trident II missile is estimated at a cool $40 billion, but after all, as the submarine fleet commander points out, it will "serve as a defense against terrorism, drug trade, and other global conflicts."

"Faster, faster," said the Red Queen.